Leading Global Projects

Leading Global Projects

*For Professional and Accidental
Project Leaders*

First edition

Robert T. Moran and
William E. Youngdahl

AMSTERDAM · BOSTON · HEIDELBERG · LONDON · NEW YORK · OXFORD
PARIS · SAN DIEGO · SAN FRANCISCO · SINGAPORE · SYDNEY · TOKYO
Butterworth Heinemann is an imprint of Elsevier

Butterworth-Heinemann is an imprint of Elsevier
30 Corporate Drive, Suite 400, Burlington, MA 01803, USA
Linacre House, Jordan Hill, Oxford OX2 8DP, UK

First edition 2008

Notice
No responsibility is assumed by the publisher for any injury and/or damage to persons
or property as a matter of products liability, negligence or otherwise, or from any use
or operation of any methods, products, instructions or ideas contained in the material
herein. Because of rapid advances in the medical sciences, in particular, independent
verification of diagnoses and drug dosages should be made

British Library Cataloguing in Publication Data
A catalogue record for this book is available from the British Library

Library of Congress Cataloging-in-Publication Data
A catalog record for this book is available from the Library of Congress

ISBN: 978-0-7506-8246-6

For information on all Butterworth-Heinemann publications
visit our web site at elsevierdirect.com

Typeset by Charon Tec Ltd., A Macmillan Company. (www.macmillansolutions.com)

Printed and bound in The United States of America

08 09 10 10 9 8 7 6 5 4 3 2 1

Working together to grow
libraries in developing countries

www.elsevier.com | www.bookaid.org | www.sabre.org

ELSEVIER   BOOK AID
             International   Sabre Foundation

Contents

Foreword

The global business environments in which organizations operate have become increasingly complex and uncertain. Work has shifted from functional to project-based, from local to global. Leaders within global organizations must adapt to changing environments while orchestrating the efforts of people from diverse functional and country cultures. The rules are changing and in many cases the pace of the environmental and organizational changes eclipses individual leaders' abilities to adapt their own knowledge and skills to the new realities.

Organizations have responded to these new realities by reducing organizational layers to speed the efforts of newly empowered decision makers. They have applied matrix management to allow for more cross-functional collaboration and complex project work. Web-based technologies have enabled more and richer communication among geographically distributed team members. Theoretically these changes should create greater efficiencies and increased flexibility. However, many organizations have not fully aligned these changes with the *new* skills and knowledge required of those leading others through the new realities of our project-based world. We are asking both new and experienced leaders to translate corporate strategy into results, but many of the realities of how to bridge from strategy to results have changed. When we accept the truth that virtually all work is project work, and much of this work is global, the implications for developing leadership talent suggest new and important paths.

Some organizations have increased their emphasis on training in the fundamentals of project management. In many cases, they have required various forms of certification for project leadership positions. For certain industries, this emphasis on professionalizing project management within an organization serves as an appropriate response to dealing with complexity. At a minimum, it ensures that the certified project managers understand the fundamentals of project management. Then they learn the real work of project leadership on the job.

Our journey into the realm of global project leadership talent development began several years ago when we realized that courses in project management fundamentals were not sufficiently meeting the talent development needs of those responsible for leading complex global projects. We realized that projects were being led in all functions and geographies by individuals who did not consider themselves to be project leaders. These leaders are what Moran and Youngdahl call "accidental project leaders." They grossly outnumber the professional, or "intentional", project leaders who depend heavily on traditional project management tools and approaches.

In our organization, we identified exceptional professional project managers who lacked leadership acumen. Likewise, we identified outstanding functional leaders who were thrust into leading projects but lacked the proper skills and mindset for driving projects to completion. We also identified a need for both professional and accidental project leaders to become more adept at influencing across functional and geographical boundaries. It became clear that we needed a new hybrid leader, a global leader with a project management mindset – a *Global Project Leader*.

Global project leaders understand how their projects contribute value to their organizations. They realize that achieving strategic results, not just completing the project, is what really matters. They appreciate and understand the tools and language of project management, but they rely most heavily on the softer skills of influencing and inspiring. Global project leaders realize that influencing and inspiring across diverse functions and geographies requires broad curiosity and an interest in seeing the world through others' lenses.

This book presents thought leadership grounded in the practical realities of how to become a *Global Project Leader*. As you read each chapter, you will progress on a journey toward a deeper understanding of the skills and knowledge required to lead global projects in a rapidly changing world. We wish you well on your global project leadership journey.

Frank Waltmann
Head of Corporate Learning
Novartis
Basel, Switzerland

Acknowledgements

In our book there are three interconnected themes. One is project management. Another is leadership and the third culture. We have tried to integrate into these themes not only theory but our experiences as consultants and educators as well many ideas we heard from a large number of interviews.

For the theory we recognize the contribution of many books and articles but especially Managing Cultural Differences, 7th edition, Influencing Without Authority, 2nd edition, and Shackleton's Way. All are listed in our very short recommended readings at the end of the book.

We especially thank the many executives and managers from Novartis and American Express who generously shared with us the importance of project leadership in their organizations and the kind of training and education that would add value. Katrin Adler, a Novartis Corporate Learning Program Manager, deserves special recognition and thanks for her determination to develop leaders of global projects. She is a change agent with unflinching perseverance and commitment to talent development and coaching.

Over 1000 leaders of global projects shared their successes, challenges and failures with us and these shaped, in important ways, the organization of our book. We thank you all.

Several individuals shared very specific stories or "mini cases" illustrating examples in leading projects they experienced including Kellie Crawford, Alexander Aginsky, Emily Bealke, Dong Shi, Lara Kelso, John Huffaker, Felix Steinebrunner, and Karl Eric Leyer among others. Shigeki Yamamoto, a graduate student at Thunderbird, helped us understand Japanese non-verbal expressions of emotion and then posed illustrating same. We acknowledge and thank all.

We thank Angel Cabrera, President of the Thunderbird School of Global Management, and Beth Stoops, Executive Vice President of Thunderbird Corporate Learning, for their encouragement and support. We are appreciate and acknowledge Stephane Sinimale, Associate Director, Thunderbird EMEA, and our Thunderbird Program Manager, Marie-Laure Clisson, for their steadfast support of our work with Novartis.

In the publishing world, nothing happens without the guidance, support and feedback from the editorial team at Elsevier. We especially thank Karen Maloney, Ailsa Marks, Eleanor Blow and Naomi Robertson.

Robert T. Moran
William E. Youngdahl

Dedication

To the many leaders of global projects who shared their successes and challenges with us.
Robert T. Moran

To Lori, Tyler, and Erik for their love, inspiration, and endless source of joy in the most important of all projects – life.
William E. Youngdahl

About the Authors

 **Robert T. Moran** is a Professor of Global Management at Thunderbird School of Global Management in Arizona in the United States. He has designed and conducted executive seminars for Saudi Aramco, General Motors, Toyota, Intel, Motorola, Honeywell, Novartis, Bayer, and Singapore Airlines among many others. He has also been a faculty member in executive education programs at Babson, ESSEC (in Paris), Emory, Penn State, SMU, Stanford, MIT, and Wharton.

Virgilia and Bob are the parents of five adult children, four of whom live and work outside the United States. He has authored or coauthored 16 books.

 **William E. Youngdahl,** Ph.D., PMP, serves on the faculty of the Thunderbird School of Global Management. He has designed and delivered executive seminars for Novartis, American Express, ExxonMobil, and other organizations. He also helps organizations develop project leaders' capabilities through 360 degree feedback and serves in various corporate advisory roles. He lives with his wife and two sons in Arizona and can be reached at billyoungdahl@mac.com.

Prologue

Our book "Leading Global Projects" has three fundamental themes. We will cover the themes of leadership, culture, and project management. It is not an academic text. It is not intended to be used primarily in a classroom. It is intended as a practical/hands on/ exceedingly useful book for all leaders of, and contributors to, global projects.

Over the past 5 years, much of the material has been used by many leaders of global projects in the pharmaceutical, oil and gas as well as the financial services industries. Users have told us our material is both very relevant and very useful for their work.

During our many interviews with persons who have leadership roles on global projects, we learned that most are not "professional project managers." Only a few were certified by the Project Management Institute. Some had never read a book on project management or attended any course on the subject. These people are what we call "accidental project managers."

We believe the many skills of a highly effective leader of global projects can be clustered around three competencies.

One is the ability to influence without authority across cultures and functions. Global project leaders most often lead without formal authority. They reach across geographies and functions to work with (and often borrow) individual contributors for their projects. They are, in essence, competing against functional bosses and other project managers for the attention of people needed to do the work on their projects.

The magic of truly gifted project leaders reveals itself when people feel intrinsically compelled to work on the project. For this to happen, the project leader needs to look through the lens of the individual contributor and provide both work and rewards that do not leave the individual asking "What's in it for me?" Gifted project leaders develop reputations for fair exchanges.

Two, the skilled leader is able to create project value and strategic alignment. Global project leaders deliver project results, but they also ensure that the results deliver value to key stakeholders. They understand that the organization's strategy matters more than any individual project. They are willing to "kill" projects that no longer support organizational strategy in order to free up resources for higher priority projects.

Third, a skilled leader is able to develop and share the project vision. Global project leaders focus not only on the "what" associated with project scope but also the "why" of project purpose. Individual contributors want to know why they are working on a project. What is the purpose and how do team members and customers benefit from the involvement in creating the project output?

When project leaders understand why they are working on a project, they are more likely to prioritize the work into their daily schedule. The benefits of creating a project vision are tangible. It creates excitement about the purpose of a project and energizes project teams to deliver amazing results within the constraints of time and budget. When we look at a project that is over budget and behind schedule, team members routinely question the purpose of the project.

In several chapters, we have left a small amount of space to write responses. There is no appendix to look for the "right" answers. There are no right or wrong answers. In many organizations and on many project teams, there is a difficulty in moving from "walk to talk" or moving from "say to do" or moving from "knowledge to action". The forces to resist this movement are many and difficult to overcome. Writing one's thoughts and committing oneself to action is one way to overcome this resistance.

We are aware that most learners retain a small amount of any speech they have heard or any book they have read. For each chapter in our book we have a very straightforward and clear objective. Our goal is to have readers remember four or five points from each chapter. As four or five points are remembered, our goal is that readers will be able to use two or three of these points as they lead or contribute to a global project team. We are convinced from our experience working with hundreds of project leaders in our seminars that using these very straightforward and clear points will add value.

In the drug development area, one executive told us that reducing the development time of a new drug by even 1 week could result in the saving of lives while increasing the profits for the organization that would then allow new research investments which would have the benefit of saving more lives. Effective project leadership leads to sustainable prosperity.

In our book we are using our experiences and borrowing and reshaping other material we have written. Of particular use and value is the seventh edition of a classic book "Managing Cultural Differences – Global Leadership Strategies for the 21st Century". We also found the book, "Influence without Authority" by Allan Cohen and David Bradford very useful.

All examples are actual and real. In most instances, however, we have changed the names and in some cases the industries.

We have included a list, albeit a short list, of recommended books which readers will find valuable if they wish to pursue any topic in more detail.

Begin reading and remember our goal for each chapter is to remember a few key points. Use several of these approaches and our guarantee is unequivocal – you will benefit personally and professionally.

Robert T. Moran, Scottsdale, Arizona 2008

William E. Youngdahl, Prescott, Arizona 2008

Leading Global Projects

Over the years, we have met a few individuals who are truly professional "project managers." Their profession and their career are as project managers. These individuals are professional project managers.

Without much exaggeration, it can be said that all work done in organizations is project work. Individuals who are involved in a project work need leadership abilities, must understand a few basics of project management, and since the world is now flat must be aware of the concept of culture and develop the skills of working in a multicultural, highly interdependent global economy. We call these individuals who are not professional project managers "accidental project managers."

Consider the situation of James who is an accidental project leader. His schedule, described shortly, is real life as are all other examples and mini cases in our book. As many, if not most project leaders are accidental project leaders, we will be introducing throughout the text some fundamentals of project management. The three threads of leadership, culture and project management, however, will be woven and stitched together throughout the chapters. In a sense, therefore, this book has relevance for most working individuals and comes with a promise that all readers will find many ideas, models, paradigms, and imperatives that will immediately help them become more effective and productive in their work.

Throughout the book we are going to be descriptive in providing some "realities" (e.g., in Chapter 1, Reality 2 states our world is global.) No one disputes this reality. We also cover some project management fundamentals (e.g., all of Chapter 2). We are also going to be "prescriptive" (e.g., the imperatives in Chapters 3 through 10). The realities and fundamentals lead to the imperatives.

The actual schedule of James who found himself looking at his travel schedule for the upcoming weeks after only 3 months with a large consumer electronics company.

Shanghai – Travel Sunday 14th, Monday–Friday
- Introductions
- Meet with Kannan Rao and IT team (Monday/Tuesday)

- Align strategy w/corp. TNG team (Wednesday/Thursday)
- Shanghai facilities overview (Thursday/Friday)

India – Travel Saturday 20th, Sunday 21st, Monday 22nd
- Introductions
- Facilities overview
- Meet with Ravi Kumar
- Discuss LPT and overall impact to PDG strategy
- TLP to manage 3PL network in India
- Challenges and opportunities

Japan – Travel Tuesday 23rd, Wednesday 24th, Thursday 25th
- Introductions
- Facilities overview
- Meet with Matsu San, SCM
- Discuss TMS and overall importance to FPG strategy
- TMS to manage network in Japan
- Discuss challenges and opportunities

Korea – Friday 26th, Saturday 27th
- Introductions
- Facilities overview
- Meet with Mr. Kim and Mr. San
- Discuss TMS and overall importance to ALP strategy
- Discuss challenges and opportunities

Shanghai – Travel Sunday 28th, Monday–Friday
- Tuesday/Wednesday – Workshop
- Thursday open to visit intra-China plants
- Look for apartment

One would think from glancing at the schedule that James is a rather senior manager. In fact, James is quite junior in the organization. His assignment was to spearhead an initiative in which his company would replace an endless list of transportation and logistics providers with a single third-party logistics provider worldwide.

The overarching goal of this travel schedule was to obtain buy-in for an initiative to consolidate logistics from a dizzying array of providers spread across the world to a single third-party logistics provider that would offer various logistics and supply chain functions for the company on a global basis. We talked with James before he departed on this trip to get some sense of his feelings about the assignment. What he told us was quite revealing and not so different from the stories we hear from those managing projects in companies around the world.

1. An initiative/project was handed to James.
2. James had to make sense of the initiative in a limited period of time.
3. James was responsible for driving the initiative to completion but he had very limited formal authority.
4. James had to influence effectively across country, division, and functional cultures.

Accidental Project Managers

James was not given the official title of project manager. He's just like millions of us given a tough assignment and told implicitly or explicitly to figure it out and get it done. We have found in our 40 years of combined experience working with thousands of executives in training seminars that most projects are not managed by project managers. Many projects are not even called projects. We hear labels like initiatives, strategic priorities, new product offerings, new services, and the like. The world is full of "accidental" project managers leading significant projects and initiatives.

James conducted some research into what needed to be done and what was driving the initiative. Through discussions with his boss and other supply chain subject matter experts, James discovered that there was almost no visibility as to how much was really being spent on transportation and logistics. Part of this had to do with differences in the way overhead expenses were allocated and reported at dozens of plants around the world. From various sources, James was beginning to hear that some of the plant managers throughout Asia were hiring their relatives to provide logistics and transportation services and that these costs were intentionally obscured in the accounting systems.

James knew that this would not be an easy project. He was hopeful that the Asian plant managers would respond favorably to him despite his relatively junior status since he was coming from corporate. That said, James admitted to making some early mistakes. "I realized after my telephone conversation with a purchasing manager in Japan that I should not have defaulted to using their first names so quickly. It would have been much more appropriate to have used Siguro-San."

Like so many initiatives in global organizations, James' project would require the following skills:

- An ability to demonstrate the strategic contribution of simple, complex, and ever evolving projects.
- Cross-cultural acumen to understand work effectively across cultures (e.g., Americans and Chinese) and across functions (e.g., marketing and manufacturing).
- An ability to influence and motivate without formal authority.
- Adaptability and skillfulness in leading people through change.

We broadly define the challenge of global project leadership along the three themes of strategic project management, cross-cultural effectiveness, and project leadership. We need to be able to communicate to all stakeholders, (our bosses and colleagues) on a strategic level how our projects contribute value. We need to effectively communicate and lead across country cultures as well as functional cultures or different company cultures. In some cases we even need to deal with the cultures of governments and nongovernmental organizations. When these competencies are "within the triangle model" success is likely. If the competencies are not within the triangle, they will have to be learned or the project will inevitably fail (Figure 1.1).

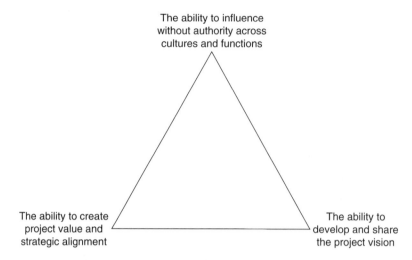

The ability to influence
without authority across
cultures and functions

The ability to create
project value and
strategic alignment

The ability to
develop and share
the project vision

Figure 1.1   Summary of Youngdahl–Moran Model.

Global Project Leadership Imperative

We live in an increasingly project-based world full of projects, initiatives, task forces, globally distributed teams, offshoring, outsourcing, and all of the increased multitasking that goes along with an increasingly complex business landscape. At its most basic level, a *project is a temporary endeavor aimed at achieving some unique set of outcomes that meet or exceed the needs and expectations of our key project stakeholders.* Unless we are directly supervising individuals performing routine operations, we are likely working on multiple initiatives that fit the definition of a project. Even if our job does have a routine component, it is likely that we are still bombarded by the need to participate in various initiatives and projects. We have not worked with many individuals who are not overworked and given lots to do.

If you need further convincing that we live in a project-based world, take stock of your own calendar and ask yourself the following questions:

- What percentage of my time am I spending supporting various initiatives and projects?

- Considering all of the initiatives or projects, how much of my time am I spending collaborating with people from different functional areas or different countries?

We are finding that executives, managers, and subject matter experts working in multinational organizations routinely answer that they are spending 75% or more of their time working on a portfolio of large and small projects and initiatives with extensive cross-functional and cross-cultural collaboration. Given the proliferation of global projects, understanding how to communicate the value of global projects and then lead complex global projects with geographically distributed team members and other stakeholders has become a required skill for global project leaders.

Getting Strategic About Global Projects

Strategy, at its essence, is the process of formulating a set of objectives and then deciding on how we will achieve the objectives. Projects execute strategy. Quite simply, we can look to the portfolio of projects to gain an understanding of where we are heading as an organization. If we can't make sense of our portfolio of projects, then we either have a problem with our strategy or with the selection of projects aimed at achieving our strategic objectives.

While we do not necessarily suggest that all organizations adopt formal project portfolio management, we do argue for developing a strategic project management mindset. A strategic project management mindset begins with the realization that we have too many project ideas and not enough people, time, and budget to act on every idea for a new project or initiative. That said, we need to find a way to prioritize and select the right projects based on the appropriate balance of attractiveness and risk. Once we have prioritized our projects, we budget and resource the most important project first followed by lower-ranked projects until we run out of budget.

The essence of the strategic project management mindset is to realize that strategy is more important than the project. As project managers, we are taught to deliver project results. As global project leaders, we need to focus on delivering project value. We could successfully complete a project without delivering value because our strategy has changed or because we hadn't really thought through the connection between the project and the organization-level strategy in the first place.

Consider the case of the Millennium Dome project. The project was conceived in the mid-1990s by John Major's Conservative party in England, and then continued under Tony Blair's Labour party. The original idea was to create a large dome, supported by private capital from exhibitors, on the Greenwich Peninsula in the Docklands area of eastern London to celebrate the country's third millennium. The project, with the budgeted cost of £449 million, was completed at £728 million. It was considered a financial flop not only because it was significantly over budget but also since there were not enough private companies interested in setting up exhibits within the Dome.

In 1997, Tony Blair's government took over the Millennium Dome project. In the previous year, John Major's government took the decision to establish public rather than private funding for the project. This major signal that the commercial value of the Dome to private investors did not merit continuing with the original scope of using the Dome as an exhibition center could have led to project termination or significant restructuring. Instead, Blair, fueled by optimistic visitor forecasts, continued the project.

The Dome opened to the public in January, 2000. By December 31, 2000, the Dome was closed to the public after attracting just over 6 million visitors, about half the original estimate. In 2001, the Dome was sold to Meridian Delta Limited for conversion to a 20,000 seat sports and entertainment venue. In winter of 2003, the Dome was used for a Winter Wonderland 2003 experience. During the Christmas holiday season in 2004, it was used to house the homeless.

Global Project Leadership Reality 1

Today's global projects are tomorrow's strategic results.

Getting strategic about projects requires us to keep our eyes, first and foremost, on the strategy. Strategies might change over time based on business circumstances, politics, or the economy. We have to have the courage to terminate the "walking dead" projects in our organization and question the value of all of our projects, even as we are championing them.

The Cultural Context of Project Leadership

It was the great French philosopher–mathematician Pascal who said that "there are truths on this side of the Pyrenees that are falsehoods on the other." Leaders of global projects must not be "ethnocentric." How can one successfully communicate if one judges another culture's customs as foolish, ridiculous, or not quite as good as one's own? Skillful project leaders have learned to see the world differently and understand the way others manage and do business. This implies that there is no single way of doing anything and that no one culture has "truth by the tail." A Swedish executive of a large multinational corporation expressed it this way: "We Swedes are so content with the quality of our products and the Swedish way that we forget that 99% of the rest of the world isn't Swedish."

We have taught in one global business school for a combined total of over 40 years. Each year we travel over 100,000 miles in our work. The graduate student body at our institution is over 50% foreign nationals from over 60 different countries. Our classroom discussions are filled with different and very creative approaches to global business issues. Diversity abounds (Figure 1.2).

We have also worked closely with many hundreds of leaders of global projects, and thousands of mid-level to upper-level managers, and we no longer have to convince any leader or member of a global project team that "culture counts." Everyone has many

Mostly
similar

Mostly
different

Figure 1.2   Cultures in Contact Continuum.

examples of the challenges of working skillfully across cultures. Most have examples of costly mistakes. But how culture counts and the skills project leaders need to get alignment, understand the root of any problem and celebrate small and large successes is a challenge for many.

What is "Culture"

Anthropologists, sociologists, psychologists, and many others use the word culture in their writing, research, and teaching. There are hundreds of definitions of culture in the published material. Our definition is: Culture is the way we do things here. Culture includes *behavior*. An example of behavior related to culture is that in Japan most people use chopsticks when eating. In India and many other countries they use their right hand. Using a knife, fork, and spoon to eat is not a universal behavioral custom for eating.

Culture also includes *values*. A value is learned very early and is at the basis of many behaviors. An example of a value is punctuality. The Germans, Swiss, Scandinavians, and others are very punctual. They arrive on time to attend a meeting. Latin Americans however do not have the same value of punctuality and time is perceived somewhat differently. Arriving "on time" depends on what "on time" means. Preserving harmony in relationships is also a value. When societies value harmony in relationships, conflict is often avoided or found very difficult.

Assumptions are also a part of culture. Assumptions such as "people are basically good" versus "people are fundamentally evil" and will take advantage whenever they can is an example of an assumption. Assumptions also influence behavior.

Culture most often refers to national culture. When we refer to the Japanese, Chinese, Swiss, Brazilians, Saudi Arabians, and Canadians we mean national culture. However, within a national culture there are also many subcultures. In the United States, for example, there are subcultures of Native American and within the Native American community there are many tribes. One can also look at culture from the perspective of organizational or corporate culture. The culture of Novartis, a large Swiss pharmaceutical company, is in a number of ways different from Pfizer, a large US-based pharmaceutical company. The corporate culture of Exxon Mobil is different than the culture of Shell. The culture of General Motors is different than the culture of Toyota. And within each organization there are also unique and specific functional cultures such as a legal department, human resources, marketing, engineering, development, or manufacturing. Each of these departments or divisions or units share certain things in common with the organization, but also has unique aspects.

Culture is all pervasive and very complex. Certain aspects change quite easily while others move only at a glacier pace.

The following 10 aspects are important for any leader of global projects to be aware of. These aspects will assist a project leader who will conduct a "cultural audit" or consider "cultural due diligence" as important as a financial, technical, or product due diligence (Figure 1.3).

1. *Sense of Self*: The self-identity of an individual can be manifested, for example, by humble bearing in one culture and by macho behavior in another. Some cultures are very structured and formal, while others are more flexible and informal. Some cultures are very closed and precisely determine an individual's place, while others are more open and changing. Each culture validates self in a unique way.

- Sense of self
- Communicational language
- Dress and appearance
- Food and eating habits
- Time and time-consciousness
- Relationships
- Values and norms
- Beliefs and attitude
- Mental process and learning
- Work habits and practices

Figure 1.3 Components of Culture for Cultural Audit.

2. *Communication and Language*: The communication system, both verbal and nonverbal, distinguishes one group from another. The meaning given to gestures often differ by culture. In this chapter we will develop the idea of "low/high context communication," which is at the root of many communication misunderstandings.

3. *Dress and Appearance*: This includes the outward garments and adornments that tend to be culturally distinctive. We are aware of the Japanese kimono, the African headdress, the Englishman's bowler and umbrella, the Polynesian sarong, and the Native American headband.

4. *Food and Feeding Habits*: The manner in which food is selected, prepared, presented, and eaten often differs by culture. Americans love beef, yet it is forbidden to Hindus, while the forbidden food in Muslim and Jewish culture is normally pork, eaten extensively by the Chinese and others.

5. *Time and Time Consciousness*: One's sense of time differs by culture. Generally, Germans are precise about the clock, while many Latins are more casual. In some cultures, promptness is determined by age or status. Thus, in some countries, subordinates are expected on time at staff meetings, but the boss is the last to arrive.

6. *Relationships*: Cultures determine human and organizational relationships by age, gender, status, wealth, power, and wisdom. The family unit is the most common expression of this characteristic, and the arrangement may go from small to large. In a Hindu household, the joint family may include under one roof, mother, father, children, parents, uncles, aunts, and cousins. In fact, one's physical location in such houses may also be determined, with males on one side of the house, females on the other. There are some places where the accepted marriage relationship is monogamy, while in other cultures it may be polygamy or polyandry (one wife, several husbands).

   In some cultures, the authoritarian figure in the family is the head male. In other cultures, the elderly are honored, whereas in others they are ignored. In the Arab world, many women must wear veils and appear deferential to men, while in others the female is considered the equal of the male.

7. *Values and Norms*: From a culture's value system norms of behavior are determined for that society. Values influence conventions as expressed in gift-giving, rituals for birth, death, and marriage, guidelines for privacy, showing respect or deference, and expressing good manners.

8. *Beliefs and Attitudes*: People in all cultures have concerns for the supernatural that is evident in their religions and religious practices. Western culture is largely influenced by the Judeo–Christian–Islamic traditions, while Eastern or Asian cultures have been dominated by Buddhism, Confucianism, Taoism, and Hinduism.

9. *Mental Process and Learning*: Anthropologist Edward Hall proposed that the mind is internalized culture, and the mental process involves how people organize and process information. Germans stress logic, while the Japanese and the Navajo reject the Western idea of logic. Some cultures favor abstract thinking and conceptualization, while others prefer rote memory and learning.

10. *Work Habits and Practices*: Another dimension of a group's culture is its attitude toward work. Work has been defined as exertion or effort directed to produce or accomplish something. Some cultures espouse a work ethic in which all members are expected to engage in a desirable and worthwhile activity. For some cultures, the worthiness of the activity is narrowly measured in terms of the income produced.

These 10 general classifications are a basic model for understanding important aspects of a culture and as a leader of a global project for conducting a "cultural audit." A cultural audit is a way to determine how culture may be an advantage or a challenge. More sophisticated "tools" for conducting such an audit will be discussed in subsequent chapters.

A "Cultural" Mistake

Many years ago, one of the authors of this book assisted the Japanese Skating Union as an ice hockey coach in preparation for the 1972 Winter Olympic Games, which were to be held for the first time in Asia. At a team meeting, he announced that he was changing a player in one of the forward lines.

That evening after the game (and we won the game) he was told that his decision was not a correct one because "all three players on the forward line had graduated from the same university." He asked himself, "What does graduating from the same university have to do with playing ice hockey?"

He learned that in Japan graduating from the same university does have something to do with one's ability to play hockey and score goals. By changing a player he disrupted the harmony and relationships among the team members. His lesson was that he must spend more time as a coach (leader) of a project (be able to play against the best teams in the world) in understanding the people he was working with.

A few years later the same author was invited to participate as a consultant to a global project review of a large US high technology company. The president and his direct reports were present. After exchanging a few pleasantries, the president went to a blackboard, grabbed a stub of chalk, and with one bold gesture drew a horizontal line about 3-feet long. At one end of the line he wrote in large letters "TERMINATE," and at the other end of the line "MAKE THEM DO WHAT WE WANT." He then came to the consultant and said, "You're an expert, give us your advice."

The consultant thought for a minute about the purpose of the meeting. Obviously the president had reached a crossroads and wanted to make a choice. The consultant went to the blackboard and said I have a third alternative. He wrote, "Why not develop your skills as leaders of global projects."

Denial

It has been demonstrated in studies and sophisticated research that many "deny realities." In families, children deny that their parents are alcoholic, women deny that their husbands are abusive. In business organizations and academic institutions, similarly, "realities" are suppressed, "feelings" are stuffed and intellectualization exercises force new realities into old paradigms. We build mental worlds of "shoulds" and "might have beens."

Denial is also a problem for leaders of global projects. The following parody illustrates denial in a humorous way. The example is American but it can easily apply to any global project when changes in scope, cost, timelines, or any other dimension is ignored or denied.

The American Way

The Americans and the Japanese decided to engage in a competitive boat race. Both teams practiced hard and long to reach their peak performance. On the big day they both felt ready.

The Japanese won by a mile.

Afterward, the American team was discouraged by the loss. Morale sagged Corporate management decided that the reason for the crushing defeat had to be found, so a consulting firm as hired to investigate the problem and recommend corrective action.

The consultant's findings: The Japanese team had eight people rowing and one person steering; the American team had one person rowing and eight people steering.

After a year of study and millions spent analyzing the problem, the consulting firm concluded that too many people were steering and not enough were rowing on the American team.

So, as race day neared again the following year, the American team's management structure was completely reorganized. The new structure: four steering managers, three area steering managers, one staff steering manager, and a new performance review system for the person rowing the boat to provide work incentive.

The next year the Japanese won by two miles.

Humiliated, the American corporation laid off the rower for poor performance and gave the managers a bonus for discovering the problem.

Source: Unknown

In our work with leaders of global projects we no longer have to convince them that "culture counts."

Two Typical Leaders of Global Projects

The following are typical examples of leaders of global projects today. Frederick is highly skilled technically with very little global experience and is only beginning to have a leadership role in a project. Giuseppe is also highly skilled technically (both Frederick and Giuseppe have PhD's from prestigious universities), is multilingual and very experienced in the global arena.

Frederick is a successful employee who is much admired by his colleagues for his ability in the lab. His frank, open, and uncompromising manner has earned him a great deal of respect as a team player on project development teams. He had no experience in Asia and only very little knowledge of the business culture of Japan when he was sent there to share technology and processes he helped develop. He received his first passport prior to leaving for Japan.

Giuseppe was born in the Italian speaking part of Switzerland and raised in a predominantly Italian cultural environment. Switzerland is a multicultural society. The Swiss influences are marked, and make a Swiss Italian different from a pure Italian. He learned French and German at school. He is multilingual, has lived in two countries other than Switzerland for more than 5 years and has been a top performer in leading several global projects.

Let us now look at additional global project leadership realities for these two individuals as they lead a global project.

Global Project Leadership Reality 2

Our world is "global" and the rest of the world is not hoping to "become" American, or Swedish or British or Chinese. Most are quite satisfied with who they are.

There are approximately 6.4 billion people on earth. Too many for us to imagine.

Aberley suggests if there were only 1000 people in the world (we can imagine this) it would include: 584 Asians, 124 Africans, 150 eastern and western Europeans and former Soviets, 84 Latin Americans, 52 North Americans, and 6 Australians and New Zealanders. It is a global world and most countries are only a small part. The world has also changed in the past 15 years in many important ways.

Thomas Friedman posites the world is also "flat." In his book *The World is Flat* he states:

> In 1492 Christopher Columbus set sail for India, going west…he called the people he met "Indians" and came home and reported to his king and queen. "The world is round." I set off for India 512 years later…I went east…I came home and reported only to my wife and only in a whisper: "The world is flat."

But what does this mean to leaders of global projects. Friedman quotes Nilekani, the Chief Executive Officer of Infosys Technologies Limited whose headquarters are in Bangalore, India. The result for project leaders is that many project teams are "virtual"…and much more challenging to lead effectively. Nilekani says:

> Outsourcing is just one dimension of a much more fundamental thing happening today in the world'. "What happened over the last (few) years is that there was a massive investment in technology…At the same time computers became cheaper and dispersed all over the world, and there was an explosion of software-e-mail, and proprietary software that can chop up any piece of work and send one part to Boston, one part to Bangalore, and one part to Beijing, making it easy for anyone to do remote development. – and this gave a whole new degree of freedom to the way we do work, especially work of an intellectual nature…

Our world is "global"*and* "flat." We are happy to be of our own culture but the "flattening of the world" through technology and other factors has connected us in ways we could have never imagined.

Culture is Learned

Culture is learned and individuals from the same culture have similar but not exactly the same learning experiences. We can express it this way. Psychologists, anthropologists, and others from around the world generally agree that:

1. An individual's early childhood experiences exert a strong effect on one's personality. The points in debate are twofold. What are the critical experiences and by what age is our "basic personality" formed?
2. Similar early experiences tend to produce similar personality types in the children who experience them.
3. The child rearing and socialization practices of any culture are patterned and tend to be similar but not identical for families in the same culture. One of the authors returned recently from East Africa where he spent time among the Maasai and observed great similarity in the way Maasai mothers related to their children.
4. Finally, child rearing practices vary from culture to culture.

Culture is learned and all persons are "programmed" – we all carry a "cultural DNA."

We believe if a Chinese baby would have been adopted by one of our families, the Chinese baby would look Chinese and behave like our children. Conversely, if one of our children would have been adopted by a Chinese family, he or she would look like us, speak perfect Mandarin, and behave like the other children in the Chinese school.

Culture is learned but all we "see" is behavior. To understand the "why" or the "meaning" of behavior that we observe in leading global projects, we must take into account:

1. The culture of the individual.
2. The personality of the individual.
3. The context where the behavior takes place.

Consider the following situation developed by a research organization (HUMRRO) in Washington, D.C. to test this model of human behavior. What is the best clue, a, b, c, or d, that the tourist is "American?" Remember all we see is behavior.

A tourist, while visiting an historical monument in Washington DC the country's capital, asks the guide

a.   to explain a strange looking inscription noticed in a remote corner,
b.   where to sit down and rest a while,
c.   where to get a drink of water,
d.   how tall the monument is.

This answer is d because in the US culture there is an emphasis on quantity or size.

Here is another example cited by Samuel Huntington in his book *Culture Matters.*

In the early 1990s I happened to come across economic data on Ghana and South Korea in the early 1960s, and I was astonished to see how similar their economies were then. These two countries had roughly comparable levels of per capita GNP; similar divisions of their economy among primary products, manufacturing, and services; and overwhelmingly primary product exports, with South Korea producing a few manufactured goods. Also, they were receiving comparable levels of economic aid. Thirty years later, South Korea had become an industrial giant with the fourteenth largest economy in the world. … No such changes had occurred in Ghana, whose per capita GNP was now about one-fifteenth that of South Korea's. How could this extraordinary difference in development be explained? Undoubtedly, many factors played a role, but it seemed to me that culture had to be a large part of the explanation. South Koreans valued thrift, investment, hard work, education, organization, and discipline. Ghanaians had different values. In short, culture counts.

Global Project Leadership Reality 3

Culture is learned.

Culture is Complex

Culture is like an iceberg, if you accept this analogy we believe about one-tenth of culture is visible and above the surface and about nine-tenths is below the surface and invisible (Figure 1.4).

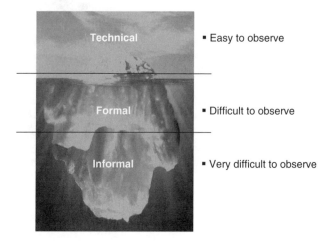

Figure 1.4   Culture Is Like an "Iceberg."

Some writers refer to the *technical* level of culture as the part of the iceberg that is visible. The technical aspects of a culture can be taught, and there is little emotion attached to this level. Project leaders operate at the technical levels of culture when discussing the chemistry of a drug or the engineering aspects of a bridge.

The *formal* level of culture is partially above and partially below sea level. We learn aspects of our culture at the formal level by trial and error. The emotion at the formal level of culture is high and violations can result in negative feelings about the violator even though the violation is often unintentional. It is difficult to admit when the violated rule is local (i.e., an aspect of one culture and not another) and therefore does not apply to everyone.

The following is a recent example shared by a person in one of our seminars. It involves a leader of a global project team with British and French scientists.

A friend of mine who works now in a small enterprise providing services to pharmaceutical companies is running crazy now with the attitude of her French coworkers. She is English but most of her staff is in Lyon (France) and every time she organizes an important meeting with potential new customers she is frustrated to see her team showing up dressed in very "creative" ways, looking more like a bunch of hippies/alternative scientists than professionals...She is convinced that this dress code impacts negatively on their chances of success at least with Germans, English and the like, so she tried to persuade her French colleagues to a more business-like attire but is encountering fierce resistance.

The informal level of culture lies below "sea level," where actions and responses are automatic and almost unconscious. Informal rules are learned through a process called modeling. Emotion is usually intense at the informal level when a rule is broken and the relationship between the persons involved is affected. Violations are interpreted personally.

A brilliant European researcher, Geert Hofstede, in his classic article "Motivation, Leadership and Organization: Do American Theories of Management Apply Abroad?" (Organizational Dynamics, Summer 1980), has identified several dimensions of national character that are below the surface of the cultural iceberg.

1. *Power Distance*: indicates "the extent to which a society accepts that power in institutions and organizations is distributed unequally."
2. *Uncertainty Avoidance*: indicates "the extent to which a society feels threatened by uncertain or ambiguous situations."
3. *Individualism*: refers to a "loosely knit social framework in a society in which people are supposed to take care of themselves and of their immediate families only."*Collectivism*, the opposite, occurs when there is a "tight social framework in which people distinguish between in-groups and out-groups; they expect their in-group (relatives, clan, organizations) to look after them, and in exchange for that owe absolute loyalty to it."
4. *Masculinity*: with its opposite pole, *femininity*, expresses "the extent to which the dominant values in society are assertiveness, money and material things, not caring for others, quality of life, and people."

Hofstede showed the position of 40 countries on the power distance and uncertainty avoidance dimension (Figure 1.5).

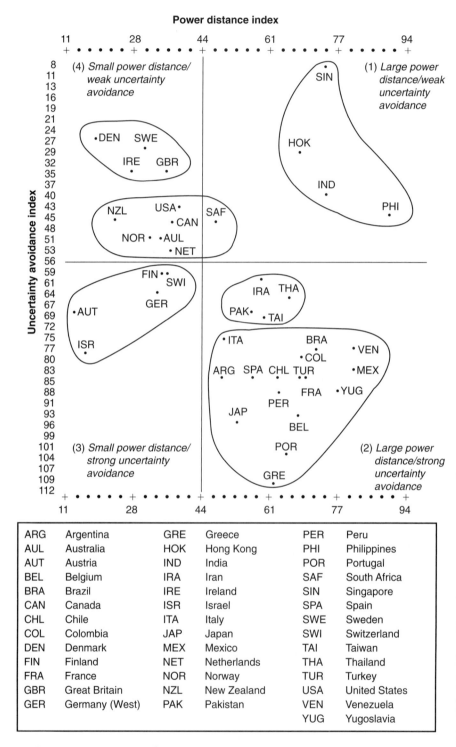

Figure 1.5 Positions of 40 Countries on the Power Distance and Uncertainty Avoidance Scales. From Cultures Consequences: International Differences in Work Related Values. Beverly Hills, Sage Publications, 1984

Global Project Leadership Reality 4

Culture is complex. Leaders of global projects need to dig deep and understand that much of what is "cultural" is hidden.

Over the years we have learned many lessons from project teams. We have concluded the following. When everything or most things are going smoothly on the team, in ideal conditions and circumstances, all or most members of the team listen to and learn from each other. When the team or individuals are under *stress* or pressure, all or most fall back on what they have learned first and believe in more strongly.

Andre Laurent discovered this in his research. In a multi-company sample of global managers in response to a number of questions, he found significant difference in their belief. Consider the following. Managers from 12 different countries were asked to what extent, along a continuum of 0–100% do you agree that, "It is important for a manager to have at hand precise answers to most of the questions subordinates may raise about their work?" The following Figure 1.6 were the managers responses.

The differences are obvious but this data is from managers from different countries who DO NOT WORK WITH EACH OTHER. Suppose French managers and American managers who work together are asked the same question namely, "It is important for a manager to have at hand precise answers to most of the questions that his subordinates may raise about their work." In Figure 1.7 in a multi-company sample on the right you can see the different opinion between the French and the Americans.

The corporate culture literature at least seems to suggest that when different people work with each other they mutually benefit and synergies occur – and there is convergence in belief on how to work together.

The results shown in Figure 1.7 surprisingly shows divergence. When we experience stress and pressure we fall back on what we have learned first which is our national culture. And we are more

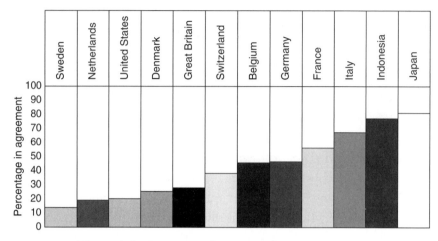

Figure 1.6   Responses of Managers from 12 Countries.
Source: Unpublished paper, Andre Laurent, INSEAD, Fontainbleau, France, 1981.

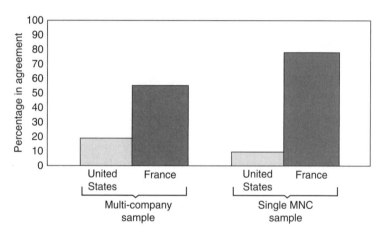

Figure 1.7   Responses of French and American Managers in Two Conditions.
Source: Unpublished paper, Andre Laurent, INSEAD, Fontainbleau, France, 1981.

convinced of its correctness. John Naisbitt summed it up succinctly. "In short, the Swedes will become more Swedish, the Chinese more Chinese. And the French, God help us, more French."

Global Project Leadership Reality 5

Culture "trumps" everything.

Understanding and Communication

Why such a strong emphasis on culture in a book on project leadership? The answer should be clear by now. Global markets for products, service, labor, and enabling technology have led to an increased dependence on global projects and initiatives. In our work with many organizations and hundreds of project leaders, we have yet to hear that projects fail due to inadequate scheduling software. Clearly, albeit anecdotal, most projects fail due to communication problems and lack of understanding.

If the person sitting across the table from us is nodding yes during a discussion about project scope but yes may not really mean yes, the basics of managing scope, schedule and cost deteriorate rapidly. The fundamentals of project management, as described in Chapter 2, are quite straightforward. The ability to seek understanding by understanding cultural differences and being willing to view project interactions and communications through another's lens separates global project leaders from otherwise highly capable project managers.

Communication is defined as the process by which persons share information meanings and feelings through the exchange of verbal and nonverbal messages. The following statements regarding communication are relevant for the project leader.

- *No matter how hard one tries, one cannot avoid communicating.* All behavior in human interaction has a message and communicates something.
- *Communication does not necessarily mean understanding.* Even when two individuals agree that they are communicating or talking to each other, it does not mean that they have understood each other.
- *Communication is irreversible.* One cannot take back one's communication, although sometimes we wish one could. Once communicated the message is part of a shared experience that influences present and future meanings.
- *Communication occurs in a context.* One cannot ignore the context of communication that occurs at a certain time, in some place, using certain media.

- *Communication is a dynamic process.* Communication is not static and passive, but rather it is a continuous and active process without beginning or end.

Anthropologist Edward T. Hall in researching the connection between words and meanings in a different language made a distinction between high and low context cultures, and how the *context* impacts communications. A high context culture uses high context communications: information is either in the physical context or internalized in the person with less communicated in the explicit words or message. Japan, Saudi Arabia, Spain, and China are cultures engaged in high context communications. On the other hand, a low context culture employs low context communications: most information is contained in explicit codes, such as words, Germany, Sweden, and the United States are cultures that engage in low context communication.

When communicating with individuals in our own culture, we can more readily assess the communication cues so that we know when our conversation, our ideas and words, are being understood and internalized. When communicating across cultures, communication misunderstandings can often occur.

The following two examples illustrate the differences between high and low context communication.

Example One: Mr. Sim's Invitation

Question: "Do you think Mr. Sim will be able to come to the course next week as I would like to make hotel reservations for him and the hotel is quite full?"
Answer: "It is possible he may have to attend a meeting in Shanghai."

Follow up question 2 days later and before the course begins.

Question sent by e-mail: "I am following up my earlier conversation and am wondering if Mr. Sim will be attending the course?"
Answer by e-mail: "As I told you previously he will NOT attend."

Result: A significant misunderstanding between the Chinese HR director and the Westerner. The HR director ignored the Westerner at work for several days.

Example Two: Avianca Crash

This is the transcript of the conversation between the captain, copilot, and controller on an Avianca flight (Avianca is the national airline of Colombia) that crashed on Long Island in 1991 (FAA Documents).

Captain to Copilot: "Tell them we are in emergency."
Copilot to Controller: "We are running out of fuel…"
Controller: "Climb and maintain 3000."

Copilot to Controller: "Uh, we're running out of fuel."
Controller: "I'm going to bring you about 15 miles northeast and then turn you back …Is that fine with you and your fuel?"
Copilot: "I guess so."

The jet ran out of fuel and crashed.

There was a misunderstanding between the copilot who was Colombian (native language Spanish – high context), and the American controller, who was a low context communicator. "Emergency" is low context. "We are running out of fuel" is more high context (as all airplanes, once they take off, are running out of fuel). The controller's last question, "Is that fine with you and your fuel?" is more high context. What does "fine" mean?

The controller could have asked, "Are you declaring a fuel emergency?" If the controller had asked this question, perhaps the copilot would have responded "yes" because he or she had just heard the pilot say, "Tell them we are in emergency."

Leaders of global projects MUST be bilingual in low and high context communication. When discussing the scope and the budget of project, low context communication is necessary. When getting to know the team, problem solving or reconstructing damaged relationships, high context communication is important.

Global Project Leadership Reality 6

Perfect communication can result in total misunderstanding.

The "Hard" Soft Skills of Project Leadership

The authors believe that the hard skills (finance, manufacturing, science) are exceedingly important for leaders of global projects. We refer to these as the "technical" skills. We choose to call the "soft" skills the "hard" skills, meaning that it is actually harder to get the soft skills right then to master the technical aspects of project management.

In a study of 256 global projects, researchers asked, to what extent do projects fail because the leader and team members are lacking in "technical skills." Answer 8%. Implication – global organizations do not make many mistakes in assigning people to work on global projects on the basis of their technical skills.

The next question asked was, "to what extent do projects fail because the leader and team members do not adapt to the external environments in which the global project is operationalized." Answer 15%.

The implication is that most leaders and participants in global projects are able to adapt to the external environments even when there are significant difficulties.

The final question was to what extent do projects fail because the team leaders and team members do not manage the interaction with global participants skillfully. The answer is 66%.

The total does not add to 100% as there were some items that overlapped or were not discrete. The message, however, is clear. Managing skillfully the interactions between people is key to project success.

The implication is obvious. The major challenge in leading global projects is the ability of the leader and the team members to work effectively across cultures, across functions, across geographies, and across timelines when these are required to bring the project to a successful conclusion.

Global Project Leadership Reality 7

No matter how brilliant you are technically, your effectiveness as leader depends on what are referred to as "soft" skills.

Conclusion

Leading global projects successfully is challenging and requires the best skills of the individuals involved. We presented a number of Global Project Leadership Realities that set the stage for dealing with the complexities of global project leadership. The rest of this book expands beyond these realities to provide specific knowledge and approaches for improving global project leadership effectiveness.

In this chapter, we focused largely on introducing the cultural context of project leadership. The strategic aspects of project leadership are presented largely but not exclusively in Chapter 2 in which we present a review of project management fundamentals and Chapter 3 in which we share approaches for telling the project story and learning from project stories. In Chapter 4, we extend the emphasis of this introduction by digging deeper into cross-cultural project leadership. Chapters 5 and 6 address influencing without formal authority and motivating key project stakeholders. In Chapter 7, we address the need for both taking and managing risks. We address the role of global project leaders in creating and managing change in Chapter 8. In Chapter 9, we discuss the importance of learning on both individual and organizational levels. We conclude, in Chapter 10, with a summary of key concepts for improving our effectiveness as global project leaders.

What any project manager or project leader knows is that most projects have unexpected delays, that there are changes in the project's scope and often increases in cost plus 100 other factors that make the professional world of the project leader stressful, challenging, and exciting.

The stresses, challenges, and excitement of leading a project come from often unpredictable complexities and changes. When our projects involve complex technologies and significant partnering with engineers, scientists, managers, and others from different cultural backgrounds, the stresses, challenges, and possibilities for excitement increase significantly.

By any measure when one has a leadership role in these projects the responsibility also increases. Understanding different aspects of project value, influencing without authority, cross-cultural and cross-functional aspects of project leadership, listening actively, treating all stakeholders as individuals, motivating teams, facilitating change, managing risks, creating project vision, and dealing with conflicts are essential capabilities of global project leaders.

Global Project Leadership Realities

1. Today's global projects are tomorrow's strategic results.

2. Our world is "global" and the rest of the world is not preparing to "become" American, or Swedish or British or Chinese. Most are quite satisfied with who they are.

3. Culture is learned.

4. Culture is complex. Leaders of global projects need to dig deep and understand that much of what is "cultural" is hidden.

5. Culture "trumps" everything.

6. Perfect communication can result in total misunderstanding.

7. No matter how brilliant you are technically, your effectiveness as a leader depends on what are referred to as "soft" skills.

What Every Project Leader Needs to Know About Project Management Fundamentals

We believe that there are certain project management fundamentals that should be understood by anyone leading a project or serving as a project sponsor or steering committee member. If you are already well versed in project management fundamentals including project portfolio management, scope management, risk management, schedule management, and project budgeting, you could either skip this chapter or skim it as a basic review.

Elementary approaches to explaining project management include discussions about what are projects and what are not projects. These discussions carve the world up into those who run ongoing operations and those who manage projects. Life isn't that simple. A manufacturing engineer responsible for production lines might also represent the manufacturing organization on new product development project teams. A director who runs a call center might also have to expand call center capacity by 50% in the next year, a significant project amidst the day-to-day responsibilities of running the operations. It's difficult to find an occupation with significant responsibility that does not involve managing projects.

To better understand this notion that we are really all doing project work, consider the following definition of a project:

A project is a temporary endeavor aimed at achieving some unique set of outcomes that meet or exceed the needs and expectations of our key project stakeholders.

We truly believe that business has become increasingly project based. This is especially true in this area in which initiatives and projects are being carried out by project team members spread around the world. As we have already stated, accidental project managers far outnumber intentional or professional project managers. Most people managing projects and initiatives never really intended to be project managers. For those of us who have stumbled into the world of projects, we need to recognize that we can learn a great deal from the profession of project management. In fact, we believe that some grounding in the fundamentals of project management provides a necessary, but not fully sufficient, foundation for leading global projects and initiatives.

If we can accept the fact that we live in a project-based world, we can look to the world of project managers for guidance on how to structure our thinking. In this chapter, we present some fundamental approaches and vocabulary to help people like James, described in Chapter 1, and others thrust into the reality of our project-based world. Some of the concepts presented in this chapter will be further elaborated throughout the book. Others will stand alone as building blocks for those less familiar with the basics of project management. Our aim is to provide a quick overview of the basics of project management before we delve into the more advanced concepts of project leadership and navigating across cultures.

The Strategy Connection

Projects form the bridge between strategy and results. We can have a great strategy, but if we can't plan, execute, and control projects effectively, we will never reach our strategic objectives. Through our work, we have found that the root cause of many project failures is lack of strategic clarity. Consider the case of James attempting to implement a global strategy that would consolidate global transportation and logistics into a single contract with a third-party logistics provider. In talking with James, we realized that he was not clear on the real purpose of this consolidation. What had changed in the external or internal environment that suggested the need to reassess the company's logistics and transportation capabilities? What were the strategic objectives that would be met by the project of consolidating transportation and logistics to a single third-party provider?

Without being able to communicate how a significant project contributes to the strategic objectives of the organization, James would be hard-pressed to convince plant managers in Japan and China of the benefits of switching from their reliable local transportation and logistics providers to a single mega-provider. As we'll discuss later when we delve into influencing without authority, if you can't convince me what's in it for me, you'd better at least be able to tell me what this is going to do for the organization.

Project Management Fundamental 1

Be clear on the business strategy including corporate objectives, business unit objectives, mission statements, and vision.

This simple advice helped James to understand the value that his project would provide to achieving overall corporate objectives. For example, one of the corporate objectives was to provide consistent service levels on a global basis to very large retail customers. The organization was not able to achieve this goal with so many different logistics and transportation providers. By working with a global third-party logistics provider that could contractually guarantee service levels, the project would be delivering significant customer value. Additionally, the project would generate significant cost savings and provide much better shipment visibility. Customers would be able to track their shipments through Web portals.

One approach we like to use for linking projects to strategy is the project value elevator speech. Imagine that you are in an elevator, and someone very senior asks "What kind of value is your project going to deliver?" You have about 22 seconds to respond. Before James realized the importance of linking his project to strategic objectives, he would have likely responded "We are going to save the company a lot of money and improve our ability to track shipments." This isn't too bad, and it's not far off the mark, but it doesn't reflect a keen understanding of how the project will deliver value. Imagine a different kind of response. "By consolidating with a single global third-party logistics provider, we will improve our global account management capabilities by providing global service levels and tracking capabilities. In the process, we will reduce total supply chain costs and free key leadership talent to work on revenue-generating opportunities."

Project Management Fundamental 2

Have a concise elevator value speech ready at all times.

When linking projects to strategy, it can be useful to think about the various forms of value that projects can contribute. Most forms of value can ultimately be woven into the overarching umbrella of strategic value, but it's useful to think of a full range of different value drivers for projects.

Financial Value

The most common methods of communicating financial value of projects are net present value (NPV) and expected net present value (eNPV). NPV is simply a number that takes into account the time value of discounted cash flows, both expenses and returns, over a given period of time such as 5 years. At the risk of oversimplifying NPV, bigger is better. Negative is generally unacceptable except in cases such as compliance projects in which the return of the project is penalty avoidance. Expected net present value is a more complicated approach that takes the discounted cash flows of many different possible outcomes weighted by probabilities. Other approaches such as payback period and internal rate of return models are also used by many organizations. One of the things to keep in mind is that any of these quantitative approaches that results in the hard numbers that comfort senior decision-makers are really just the embodiment of assumptions. It's important to understand the underlying assumptions and to communicate these underlying assumptions when presenting project value in the form of financial metrics.

The following additional types of customer value are provided for the purpose of considering a broad set of possibilities. These forms of value are not meant to be all-encompassing or mutually exclusive. Given the context of your organization, you might be able to develop additional categories.

Customer Value

Some projects provide direct benefits to customer service. Projects that increase customers' perceptions of value – the ratio of benefits relative to costs – fall into this category. If we consider initiatives to make something easier or more satisfying for our customers or to provide desirable new product features, we can weave customer value into our project value elevator speech.

Tactical Value

Projects that aim to increase operational efficiency, capacity, and improved process quality provide tactical value. Six Sigma initiatives, new production plants, offshoring, shared services, and similar projects provide tactical value. As with other types of projects, these initiatives might also provide significant strategic value.

Organizational Value

We recently helped an organization identify its guiding values through a process of appreciative inquiry. This process involves asking employees and customers to recount stories of excellence. This positively received exercise culminated in a set of guiding values that helped to energize the organization. Employees felt great ownership and the values resonated with customers as well. These types of projects are difficult to sell from the standpoint of NPV. They often involve a leap of faith that the organization will be more effective given the successful implementation of the project. The output of this project was a set of guiding principles, or values. The real benefit of these guiding principles was that they now serve the purpose of shaping decision-making and behaviors.

Compliance Value

Projects done for environmental and safety reasons or to comply with governmental regulations fall under the category of compliance value. For these projects, it is difficult but not impossible to calculate a financial return. Aside from corporate citizenship rationale and benefits, compliance projects tend to be done to avoid penalties. The avoidance of penalties can be quantified in terms of a savings if good assumptions can be made about the probabilities and outcomes. The important thing to remember is that certain projects just have to be done, and in this respect they can become very high priority projects with negative NPVs.

Strategic Value

In essence, all of the other forms of value ultimately contribute to strategic value. Strategic value merits separate attention since it relates directly to the mission, vision, and strategic objectives of our organization. We have to understand the strategy and have our project value elevator speech ready at all times. If we do not, then we are relegating ourselves to the position of managing projects in a vacuum. One of the key differences between a project leader and a project manager is being able to give the project value elevator speech. Project managers can talk about their projects and what they need to do next, but *project leaders* need to be able to communicate how their projects deliver value.

Competing for Scarce Resources in a Multi-Project World

Life would be grand if we could all manage a single project and have dedicated employees reporting directly to us. A more common reality is that we are managing six or eight or more projects in an environment in which we have to borrow team members on a part-time basis from functional areas. Most of these team members are working on several other projects and have full-time functional responsibilities as well. Combine that with an era of trying to get more done with fewer resources, and we have a recipe for very complex leadership challenges.

Most senior leaders with whom we have consulted tell us that they simply do not have enough resources to staff all potential projects. Additionally, the more projects that are launched the more stretched resources become. Something has to be done to prioritize projects and allocate resources according to the prioritization. Fundamentally this approach involves prioritizing projects and then summing, cumulatively, the budget requirements for the projects from top to bottom. Once the cumulative sum of the projects reaches the available budget for project work, we simply draw a red total budget line across the list and fund all of the projects above the red line.

This appears to be a relatively straightforward exercise, but the reality is that prioritizing projects based on value can be gut wrenching. In some cases it even requires fundamental changes in the culture of the organization. Consider the experience of a project leader who joined a French division of a pharmaceutical company that specializes in oncology research. Since she had significant prior project management experience, she was given a full load of research projects, about six in total, to manage. She worked as the project manager counterpart with the lead research scientists. After about 6 weeks on the job, she realized that the company had simply not allocated enough resources to the various projects. She discussed the situation with some of the senior project managers and was informed that this was simply a symptom of the company culture. They had always been expected to accomplish the impossible, and schedule slippages while "not tolerated" by senior managers were simply a reality given the limited resources.

This new project leader decided she would make a controversial recommendation to a senior decision board. She would recommend terminating, or at least placing on hold, half of her projects. Her peers sharply advised her to reconsider challenging the senior decision board. They laid it out very clearly that her best course of action would be to present optimism and dedication since they had learned the hard way that questioning the feasibility of projects resulted in unhealthy debates, and in some cases project managers would be labeled as naysayers. The new project leader was undeterred in communicating what she described as the plain truth.

Her approach involved a very straightforward analysis of the value being contributed by each of her projects. Some of her projects directly supported clinical trials while others appeared to be pet projects of senior sponsors (although she was more politically correct during the presentation). By clearly demonstrating the line of sight between the project deliverables and the overarching strategic and financial objectives of the company, she was able to demonstrate that some projects really were more important than others. Next, she demonstrated how much faster the more important projects could be completed if resources were more fully allocated according to strategic and financial priorities.

When she met with the decision board, she presented some very plain facts. If she continued to pursue all six projects, they would all come in significantly behind schedule and over budget. If however, the company were to pursue the three most strategically important projects, she could deliver these projects significantly ahead of schedule and under budget. Quite simply, the stretching of resources had resulted in gross inefficiencies and bottlenecks that were delaying projects and wasting resources. Given the ultimate objectives of oncology research, this was simply an unacceptable outcome. Not only did the decision board members not chastise the project leader, they praised her and questioned why others lacked the courage to present such a forthright case for allocating resources based on the value of projects.

A senior vice president in charge of development for the company characterized this meeting as "getting real" for the first time. He questioned why other project leaders had not been pushing back in similar ways. Being realistic about value contribution and the overall prioritization of projects allowed this company to accelerate many of their more important projects. As project leaders, we have to exhibit courage to let those developing the strategy understand that we must prioritize and resource projects according to strategic value contribution.

One of the fundamental reasons for committing to link projects to value is to avoid wasting time. We're not talking about basic time management. We're talking about wasting the kind of time and resources that impact oncology patients holding out for hope. Speak with any cancer survivor who has the opportunity to visit with patients in the waiting area of the oncologist's office once a year. This visit sharpens one's senses about the importance of time.

Although relatively few people in the world are engaged in searching for the cure for cancer, we know of no better illustration of the importance of time and the significance of wasting time than can be found in the project work of those searching for cures for diseases. The work that we have done in the area of pharmaceutical project management provides us with so many inspiring stories of the importance of time. Although most of us do not manage projects that could save lives, work of those striving to save lives serve as poignant examples of the importance of leading projects in such a way that time and resources are not squandered.

Project Management Fundamental 3

Don't waste time. It is the most precious resource.

Although this fundamental rule might apply to all forms of leadership, it is especially true for project management. While it might be easy to accept the notion of not wasting time, it's important to dig a little deeper and understand why this is so critical from multiple stakeholders' perspectives.

- *I'm not likely to do something for you tomorrow if you waste my time today (project team member).* This is especially true if you have no formal authority to make me do something, and most project leaders have no formal authority over us in the functional trenches.
- *I have multiple competing demands (project team member).* I work for six different project managers and a functional boss. If you waste my time, I probably end up having to do extra work for you and sacrifice the work that I could have been doing for my functional boss and other project leaders.
- *You still need to pay for the time (functional boss).* I need to allocate my people's time to your project whether or not they have been properly focused to achieve any results. Time is money.

- *Why do you need this additional budget (senior executive)?* I see lots of activity, but I'm not seeing results.
- *If I can't get it from you when you promised, I will go elsewhere* (customer). Don't forget about the penalty clause in our contract.
- *If I can't get it from you soon, my quality of life will disappear* (patient). What I want more than anything is quality time to spend with my family.

Senior executives at Airbus learned this lesson the hard way in 2006. The complex design of the entertainment system wiring on the Airbus A380 translated into significant production problems and costly delays. FedEx canceled orders for 10 A380s in late 2006 after Airbus announced delays of up to 2 years. Virgin Atlantic postponed its orders for 4 years in an apparent attempt to avoid the uncertainty created by the Airbus delays.

The cancellations, worth billions of euros, compounded the increased costs associated with the production delays. In 2006, Airbus won fewer orders than Boeing for the first time since 2000. While it is difficult to say what the medium-term or long-term impacts will be of these delays, the situation serves as an example of the negative impact of "wasting" time. While one would never want Airbus to rush production, the difference between estimated delivery date of production models of the A380 and an actual delivery dates reflected serious problems with the company's ability to identify and manage project risks.

The Airbus example highlights the significance of project risk in managing a portfolio of projects. Not all projects are created equal even if they promise similar value contributions. We need to consider how risky projects might be based on the overall scope of what is going to be done. The more we move into unchartered territories such as highly complex wiring systems, the greater the risk. As we are selecting a portfolio projects, it's important to consider both value contribution and risk. Bubble charts can be very useful for looking at multiple dimensions of value and risk. A very common form of bubble chart used in assessing project portfolios is depicted in Figure 2.1.

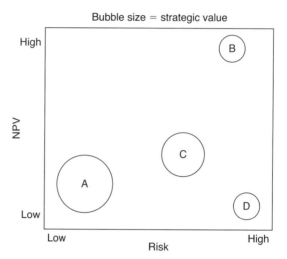

Figure 2.1 Mapping the Project Portfolio.

Broadly defined, the magnitude of risk from low to high is an indication of our assessment of the extent to which our project will encounter future problems. It is, in essence, an indication of our belief of how likely the project will achieve its stated objectives. Although there is generally a positive relationship between risk and reward, this is not always the case. Some projects, like the one depicted in bubble D, are real losers. They don't promise high financial or strategic returns, and the outcomes are highly uncertain. This process of developing bubble charts affords the opportunity to have more objective discussions about which projects make sense.

The project depicted in bubble A is likely to achieve its outcomes. It also has high strategic value despite low NPV, or financial value. Project C offers somewhat higher NPV but it is more risky. Project B would offer high financial returns, but it is very risky and based on its low strategic value it may not be a very good fit with the strategy of the business.

The process of developing bubble charts provides an opportunity for overall portfolio assessment. The aim is not to decide which project is the best. Rather, we want to take the opportunity to look at our overall portfolio of projects to ensure that we have the best mix of potential project outcomes relative to project risks. That mix will vary depending on risk tolerance and the strategic positioning of an organization.

Not all organizations implement formal portfolio management to select projects and periodically review the project portfolio to determine if projects continue to support evolving strategies. Formal project portfolio management tends to reside in companies that have a centralized project management office (PMO) and an institutionalized project management organization. We encourage organizations to strive to instill a project portfolio mindset among senior leadership and project leaders. At a minimum, senior leaders need to be thinking critically about how to select projects and periodically review the overall project portfolio.

Project Management Fundamental 4

Treat key projects as you would a portfolio of investments. Understand potential value contributions and risks.

Once we select a project based on its value contribution, we typically issue a project charter that is signed by an influential sponsor. Project charters take many forms in different organizations, but key elements of the project charter include assignment of the project manager, a description of the project, the business case, key deliverables and milestones, project assumptions, and project constraints. Some project charters also list key stakeholders, those individuals or organizations who can impact our project or who are impacted by our project.

The business case should include a succinct description of the value that will be delivered by the project. It answers the question, why are we doing this? We should be as specific as possible with respect to the benefits. If we consider James' project to consolidate transportation and logistics providers to a single third-party provider, we might have a business case that looks like this:

This project will consolidate 53 separate transportation and logistics providers spread across the world into a single provider. This decision has been taken to address concerns from large global customers that they are receiving significantly different service levels in different regions and they do not have appropriate shipment visibility. We will select a single third-party logistics and transportation provider that can guarantee consistent service levels and provide state-of-the-art Web-based shipment tracking. An additional goal of the project will be to reduce transportation and logistics costs by 10% or more.

Think of the business case as an expanded project value elevator speech. It provides clarity about why we're pursuing the project. A strong business case also ensures top leadership support. There are times when we need to go back to senior sponsors for additional resources or support in marshaling existing resources. The signed project charter serves as a contract with project sponsors to provide some assurance of support.

Project deliverables are the outcomes of the project. If we are developing a shared service operation in Budapest, for example, the overall deliverable would be a fully functioning shared services operation on a given date. In addition to the overall project deliverables, we would want to list what needs to happen at certain points in time in order to achieve the overall project deliverable. It's best to list deliverables as nouns rather than verbs. For example, "Select Site" should be replaced with "Site Selected." Although the distinction might be subtle, site selected indicates that we have completed something whereas select site describes a process rather than an outcome. We then assign due dates to deliverables to identify project milestones. Without setting clear milestones, opportunities for wasting time and resources abound.

Project Management Fundamental 5

Clearly communicate key project milestones (deliverables and dates).

Get the Assumptions and Constraints on the Table

Project assumptions are beliefs that we hold to be true. For example, a project manager in charge of creating an accounting service center in India assumed that cross-functional planning could be handled by a virtual team made up of members located in Belgium, the United States, and Costa Rica. Many of the transactional accounting functions performed in each one of these locations could be centralized in the shared services group being formed in India. This assumption that the work could be handled readily in a virtual setting via e-mail and phone proved to be unfounded. After months of disjointed communication and politicking, the project leader was given authorization to form a heavyweight team of full-time dedicated team members pulled from the different locations to work through the project in Belgium.

The project charter for this offshoring project did not include clear statements of project assumptions. By listing assumptions, we are providing an opportunity to question whether the assumption, that which we hold to be true, is really a risk that needs to be mitigated. Had the assumption about the ability of the virtual team to work together been identified and then challenged, risks could have been mitigated by collocating the team earlier or by at least allowing the group to work intensively face-to-face before attempting to work in a virtual manner. The importance of listing assumptions at the front end of projects cannot be overstated. We have seen too many projects get derailed as a result of unspecified assumptions. As project leaders, we need to spend some time thinking through project assumptions. If we are sitting on steering committees or project decision boards, we need to ask some probing questions about assumptions before approving projects and during the planning and execution phases to help project leaders uncover risks that could impact the project.

Project Management Fundamental 6

Clearly communicate and challenge key project assumptions. Assumptions might really be risks.

In addition to listing assumptions that might really be risks to be managed, identifying project constraints clarifies our options for completing our project. Constraints are any factors that limit our options in pursuing the project objectives. Budget and time constrain most projects. If we had unlimited budget and unlimited time, we could pursue any option to complete our objectives, and we wouldn't even be concerned about the clock. Other less obvious constraints include talent of team members, language capabilities, IT infrastructure, existing company policies, and the like. It's important to know what factors constrain our options so we can be realistic in the pursuit of our project objectives.

Project Management Fundamental 7

Understand the project constraints that limit our options for pursuing project objectives.

Formal project planning begins after project charter signoff. The charter signifies that the resources will be available to proceed with detailed project planning. It does not guarantee full funding for the project as it could be terminated if the organization's strategy changes or significant additional risks are identified. We have found that organizations that fail to invest time in detailed project planning spend a disproportionate amount of time rethinking project scope and reacting to events. We strongly encourage organizations to spend extra time thinking through project scope, schedule, budget, and risk management.

The Project Plan

Recall the Millennium Dome project referenced in Chapter 1. The story of the Dome illustrates the first critical role of project planning – clearly linking what we planned in terms of project deliverables and how we will achieve those deliverables to the original purpose of the project. This is formally known as scope management. In the case of the Millennium Dome project, the scope was allowed to evolve to the point that the original purpose of the Dome was all but forgotten.

Scope Management

As a practical matter, there are two types of scope, product scope and project scope. Product scope is the *what* of the project. Every project has some unique outcome. Defining that outcome with great clarity decreases the likelihood of wasting time and resources in pursuing blind alleys. Project scope is the *how* of the project. Based on the product scope, we need to determine what needs to be done and then ultimately who needs to do the work. Some organizations refer to the formal description of project scope as the statement of work. Others call it a scope statement. The important thing to remember is that the deliverables identified in the project planning phase should link to the business case and the deliverables outlined in the project charter. That said, during a formal project planning phase we go much deeper into the full set of deliverables required to achieve the overall project objectives. In project management language, we develop the entire work breakdown structure all the way to "work packages" that can be allocated to specific departments or even individuals.

Project Management Fundamental 8

Begin detailed project planning with clear formulation of what has to be accomplished (product scope) and what has to be done (project scope) to achieve project success.

The Millennium Dome project highlights the curse of scope creep and the importance of understanding the triple constraint of project management. Scope creep refers to the tendency to add to the scope of the project over time. When we allow both internal and external customers to suggest enhancements to the project deliverables or new project deliverables, we in turn create more work, more project scope to accomplish the increased product scope.

The project leader of a project that involved the major implementation of a human resource information system in a global company learned the hard way about the perils of scope creep, the process by which the deliverables of a project keep expanding. In this case, the original goal of the project was to create a common IT system that could be used throughout the corporation to perform basic human resource management transactions. When she was finally terminated, it was clear that the project scope, schedule, and budget had spun out of control.

The project leader allowed advancements in information technologies and creative ideas within the project team to let the project stray from a what "should be done" to a "what could be done" perspective. Furthermore, as the project team members pursued new technologies with great excitement, they exposed the project to a great deal of technological risk. In working with hundreds of project management professionals, we have found that most organizations struggle with reining in runaway projects. It seems to be part of being human to want to continue exploring new possibilities. This tension between exploring new possibilities and simply executing on an agreed-upon plan of action is at the heart of the triple constraint of project management.

The triple constraint suggests that there's a trade-off among scope, schedule, and budget. Scope is what we say we're going to accomplish. If the scope expands and we want to hold the project to the original schedule, we will have to spend more money on additional resources needed to complete the expanded scope. More often than not, expanding scope means expanding both the schedule and the budget.

Project Management Fundamental 9

Scope, schedule, and budget are inextricably related to one another. Remember the triple constraint of project management.

Murphy's Law tells us that if anything can go wrong it will. Some projects seem to be more plagued by Murphy's Law than others. A fundamental question we need to ask is what could go wrong with our project and what should we do to prevent things from going wrong or respond to negative events? This is the essence of risk management.

Risk Management

Overall risk assessment should begin with the bubble charts of portfolio management. It then continues with developing the project charter when we list project assumptions that may in fact be project risks. During the project planning phase we need to do a much more detailed assessment of what could go wrong in order to avoid or mitigate project risks and develop contingency plans. Doing some detailed risk assessment during scope planning can be beneficial as thoughts about what could go wrong stem from what needs to be done and how it will be done. As we look at the overall work breakdown structure of the project, we can ask ourselves what potential problems could occur that would keep us from achieving our key deliverables?

Project risks are potential future problems. How often do we find ourselves saying "We should have realized that (fill in the blank) was going to be a problem."? The world is full of should haves, could haves, and would haves. If a key contributor to our project is hit by lightning, it's unlikely that we could have predicted or prevented the event. Unless of course that key contributor was installing a lightning rod in a thunderstorm. One of our goals in project risk management is to push more unknown unknowns to known unknowns.

The owner of a consulting organization described to us a problem that he encountered in setting up a consulting project aimed at raising capital for a company in Russia. Because of the nature of the project, all but one of the team members were externally hired consultants. Most of the consultants were people who had not worked for this particular consulting organization in the past.

There started to be a lot of tension for various reasons. One consultant didn't like the fact that we were located far away from the client necessitating a long commute. Someone else didn't like the firm's meal plan. There were a lot of little things that built up over time. The net effect was that the team did not operate cohesively. As the owner of the consulting organization said, "We usually get along really well. We have a great time when we were working or socializing." But the owner realized that this team would not likely achieve its objectives. Despite attractive financial incentives, the build up of many small irritating events ultimately necessitated reconfiguring the team. Some people were let go. Others were assigned to different projects.

The time spent dealing with productivity-draining issues and the need to completely reconfigure the team increased overhead expenses, impacted the schedule, and potentially affected the client's perception of the quality of work. Fortunately, the workaround strategy of reconfiguring the team allowed the project to get back on track and achieve its objectives.

A business school decided to enter the arena of online learning during the dotcom boom. They anointed the CIO (Chief Information Officer) to become the CLO, Chief Learning Officer. Several well-qualified Web developers were hired to create the technology required to deliver both synchronous and asynchronous courses. Champagne flowed at a meeting as the leadership of the school celebrated a new era in education, and an unlimited source of revenue for the future.

Noticeably absent from the celebration were the faculty. They were busy doing what they do – teaching courses, face-to-face. Early indications revealed that faculty had no interest whatsoever in developing and delivering online education. As one professor put it, "I get a buzz from seeing the lights go on in the eyes of my students. I don't think I'd get that buzz while facilitating a chat group or an asynchronous discussion thread." The academic administrators failed to test the fundamental assumption that faculty would be interested in participating. When professors were asked to support the project, they all found reasons, such as research and teaching face-to-face classes, to allocate their capacity elsewhere. Since these tenured professors had well-defined contractual obligations, administrators were truly influencing, or perhaps failing to influence, without formal authority.

These administrators failed to recognize lack of faculty interest and commitment as a key risk, or potential future problem. Had they done so, something could have been done to explore appropriate incentives for content development and delivery before investing heavily in the technological infrastructure. They may have even decided to postpone the investment or spin the operation out of the school and develop an entirely different business model that would not depend on faculty who preferred face-to-face teaching.

In each of these projects, and countless projects across the world, not enough time was spent thinking about what could go wrong. We like to think of the process of risk assessment as one in which we try to turn unknown unknowns into known unknowns. Unknown unknowns are the surprises of projects. Consultants being annoyed by long commutes or meal plans. Faculty who thrive on face-to-face teaching not wanting to facilitate online discussion threads. When we hear these examples we wonder why those responsible for these projects didn't consider these factors that seems so obvious with 20–20 hindsight.

Spending some extra time with the team brainstorming potential problems could have easily identified these issues with the commute, the meal plan, and the resistance to a new way of teaching. There are no absolute guidelines for how long should be spent brainstorming potential future problems. Clearly, projects contributing a great deal of strategic and financial value merit more risk assessment than those delivering little value. By taking additional time to identify risks, we have the opportunity to deal with these risks more proactively to minimize impact on scope, schedule, and budget.

Project Management Fundamental 10

Spend some extra time to turn unknown unknowns into known unknowns.

Once we have a good list of known unknowns, or risk events, for each of the significant phases in our project, we can focus on one or more of the following alternatives for proactively dealing with risks:

- *Avoid the risk altogether by changing our approach*: For example, if we have identified inexperienced engineers as a risk, we might be up to avoid the risk altogether by contracting with an engineering firm that could supply experienced engineers. When we try to avoid a risk, we might create new risks in the changed approach. It's important to do another quick risk assessment any time we change the approach to completing our project work.

- *Mitigate the risk*: Risk mitigation involves doing something to reduce the probability of the risk occurring. For example, we could provide training to the less experienced engineers. When we take measures to reduce the probability of the risk, these measures such as training need to be incorporated into the actual project work so that we account for the time, resources, and budget involved in risk mitigation.

- *Develop contingency plans*: In some cases, we may not be able to mitigate risks, or we may choose to accept the risks. If the impact of the risk is even moderately high, we should consider developing a contingency plan, a Plan B in case our Plan A does not go as expected.

- *Accept the risk*: If the risk has a low probability of occurring or even a very low impact on the project if it does occur, we may choose to simply accept the risk. For example, we generally accept the risk that project team members could become ill. Rather than develop detailed contingency plans, in many cases we simply realize that we may have to develop a workaround plan if certain unlikely events occur.

- *Transfer the risk*: There are some approaches for transferring the risk from us to someone else. For example, we can by insurance policies or outsource certain components of our work. Generally speaking, transferring risk is more likely to protect financial interest than ensure the success of the project.

If we are ultimately responsible for the project outcomes, transferring risk will not likely create as much positive impact as thoughtful risk mitigation or risk avoidance.

Generally speaking, we want to avoid any risk that would have a high probability of occurring and a serious negative impact on our project. If we cannot avoid the risk altogether, the next best strategy is to put in place a detailed mitigation strategy and contingency plan. As the probability and impact decreases, we can consider accepting the risks with outlined thoughts about contingency plans. Ultimately, the extent of risk management deployed depends on risk tolerance and awareness of the potential downside impacts of risks.

It's worth noting that there is potential for upside risks as well. In other words, there can be unknown unknowns that are positive. We tend to plan for stormy weather, but it is also worth considering that we could have exceptionally good weather. If we have curtailed spending on training and development, albeit not a wise decision, due to cost cutting, we could develop a contingency plan that would call for increased training and development should revenues increase during the project lifecycle.

Now that we have addressed the challenges of developing our project value elevator speech, determining project scope, and assessing project risks so that we can develop appropriate risk management approaches, we will turn our attention to the topic of time. We've already discussed the importance of time, but we have yet to delve into the fundamentals of project time management.

Project Time Management

Once we are clear on the project scope, we need to think about the time required to complete various deliverables. A Chinese proverb, "To know the road ahead, ask those coming back." speaks volumes for the essence of project time management. Most time estimates rely heavily on the experience of project team members and subject matter experts. The most straightforward way to determine how long something will take is to review the actual historical durations of similar activities. Where this is not possible, and a great deal of uncertainty exists, we need to add extra time (buffers) and do everything within our power to reduce the uncertainty through effective risk mitigation.

In the case of the Airbus A380, the ability to estimate schedules was complicated by the complex entertainment system that had not been used in any other aircraft. When we can't "ask those coming back" how long the journey took, our estimates rely on a combination of the science of the work that needs to be done as well as the art involved in predicting how long it might take to invent new technologies and processes for producing and assembling the project deliverables. Airbus was not in the position of simply allowing the process to drive the schedule. The company had committed to delivery dates, and paid the ultimate price of losing orders for its airplanes. Since these early setbacks, Airbus has begun delivering commercial versions of the A380 with its first shipment to Singapore Airlines in October 2007, nearly 2 years late.

We will not endeavor to get into the intricacies of critical path scheduling and other detailed approaches in this brief overview. This level of detail can be left to project analysts or could be pursued through more comprehensive training in the fundamentals of project management. As an executive, manager, or project leader in charge of a significant initiative or project, we encourage you to become familiar with some of the basic terminology and challenges involved in project time management so you can ask the right questions up your project team.

Estimating How Long Something Will Take

Estimates are just that, estimates. There are different types of estimates such as top-down estimates in which we look at the entire scope of work in the aggregate and come up with an estimate of how long the entire project might take. We also have bottom-up estimates in which the time for each detailed piece of work is estimated and then the overall schedule, or network diagram, determines the project duration. Bottom-up estimates tend to be much more accurate than top-down ones. But, the cumulative effects of the uncertainties within each estimate still make our overall estimate somewhat uncertain.

When estimating how long any piece of work will take, we need to consider availability of resources, skill levels, the experience of those who provide the estimates, and many other factors. For the sake of this treatment of the topic of estimates, it's important to emphasize that gathering data from prior similar projects and relying on experienced estimators will go a long way toward avoiding schedule surprises. Additionally, taking weighted averages of pessimistic, most likely, and optimistic estimates, with most likely receiving the greatest weight, can lead to better estimates as well as an increased ability to determine probabilities of completing the project within certain time intervals. You will need to turn to a more comprehensive source on the subject of PERT scheduling to dig deeper into this topic.

The Critical Path

Once we determine the full range of activities that need to be completed in order to achieve all of the deliverables of the project, we realize that some activities can be done in parallel while others must be done sequentially. Consider the simple example of repainting a room. Paint has to dry before we can hang pictures, but one wall might dry before another so it is possible to paint and hang pictures at the same time if there are two people to do the work.

Through the use of project management software, we can develop an overall project schedule and determine critical path, or set of critical paths. If we delay any activity along the critical path, we will delay the project. Think of the set of critical path activities as the activities that have zero slack time or, in project management language, zero float. Critical path activities are the ones we focus on when we want to accelerate our project by applying additional resources (recall the notion of the triple constraint). If we spend money trying to accelerate noncritical tasks, we are still time constrained by the critical path activities.

Project Management Fundamental 11

Focus on the critical path for time-saving opportunities.

Medtronic, a company that makes pacemakers and other medical products, decided to keep uncertainty off of its critical path by allowing only proven technology to be used in its products. It essentially adopted a train schedule for its product development. If the R&D group asked for delays in product development to allow more time for its creation of new technologies, the group was told to wait for the next train.[1]

Advanced project scheduling software and simulation approaches can be used to refine project schedules and deal with uncertainty. We have found, however, that sound judgment in seeking good estimates, making good decisions about resource availability, and keeping uncertainty off the critical path to the extent possible form the underpinnings of sound project management thinking as it relates to project time management. We do not discount the importance of more sophisticated tools, but these tools in the wrong hands might provide a false sense of security.

Our final topic in covering project management fundamentals is that of project budget management. As those leading projects, most of us must accept that we have constrained resources. If we lived in a world without financial constraints, we wouldn't have to spend much time thinking about efficient approaches to getting our work done. We would have unlimited slack resources at our disposal. Most of us don't enjoy such a fantasy existence, so the importance of managing the financial aspects of our projects is at least, if not more, important than managing the schedule.

---

[1] For more on this train schedule approach at Medtronic, refer to "We've Got Rhythm! Medtronic Corp.'s Cardiac Pacemaker Business," Harvard Business School case study # 698004 by Clayton M. Christensen, 1997.

Managing the Project Budget

When we initially request a budget for our project, as outlined in the project charter, this estimate is usually based on a top-down approach. We look at the major phases and deliverables and, based on a combination of what we know from similar projects and our best judgment, arrive at an overall estimate for the project. As we obtain detailed resource requirements during the process of laying out the project schedule, we can perform more detailed bottom-up budgeting. As was the case with project scheduling, if our overall budget estimate comes from the detail of the underlying tasks to be performed and the resources required to perform the tasks, as well as any capital expenses, we end up with a better overall estimate than one derived from a quicker top-down estimate.

Financial data gathered during the execution of a project can be used to determine whether or not the project is within budget and on schedule. This process, known as earned value analysis, depends on effective tracking of the following costs:

- How much *budgeted* activity have we completed (earned value)?
- How much we have spent in total (actual cost)?
- How much we planned to spend (our budget baseline) based on the schedule baseline (planned value)?

In many accounting systems, we take a look at how much we've actually spent relative to how much we plan to spend. With earned value analysis, we add a third variable of earned value to determine how much of our actual spend is on planned activities. Earned value analysis can be best understood by examining graphs of cumulative plan costs, actual costs, and earned value as depicted in Figure 2.2.

Notice in this example that our actual costs exceed our earned value. That is, what we have actually spent in total exceeds the amount of completed budgeted project activity. Since earned value accounts for activities that are part of the planned budget, the difference between actual cost and earned value must represent some

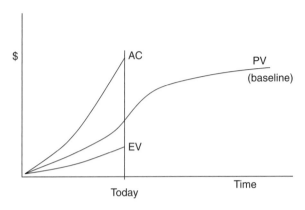

Figure 2.2 Earned Value Analysis (Over Budget and Behind Schedule).

form of waste. We've been spending money on something that wasn't part of the project plan. Simply stated, we are over budget. This is the most straightforward part of the earned value analysis, determining whether we have spent more or less than we should have spent based on the actual work completed.

Recall that planned value is the amount that we should have spent if we were precisely on time according to the baseline schedule. Our earned value, in this example, is less than the planned value. This means that the amount that we have spent on budgeted activity is less than the amount we should have spent on planned activity to date. This means, with some simplifying assumptions, that we have not completed as many activities as we planned to complete by this time. The financial data indicate that we are behind schedule. We will take a look at one more example to make sure we are clear on the concept.

Notice in the following example (Figure 2.3) that the actual cost is less than the earned value. This means that we are under budget for the work actually performed. Since the earned value is greater than the planned value, we are also ahead of schedule. With complex project networks, using cumulative project finance data can be a quick and straightforward method for determining whether or not our project is on track in terms of both budget and schedule.

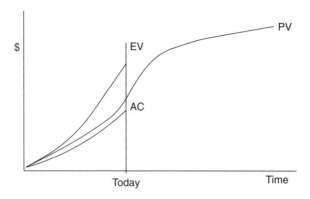

Figure 2.3   Earned Value Analysis (Under Budget and Ahead of Schedule).

Project Management Fundamental 12

Ask the tough earned value analysis questions to determine if we are within budget and on schedule.

Most organizations track total spend and total budget. To perform earned value analysis, we need to track earned value – how much we have spent on activities included in our plan. This level of sophistication can be obtained easily by using even rather basic project management software. Again, the value is not so much in the tool as it is in the understanding of the output. As executives, managers, and project leaders, some understanding of earned value analysis helps us ask the tough but necessary questions to keep our projects within budget and on schedule.

Summary

In this chapter, we presented 12 project management fundamentals. These fundamentals are not intended to represent a comprehensive overview of project management. Rather, our hope was to share some basics for those with less formal training in project management and for those in need of a quick review.

As professional or accidental project leaders, we need to begin our project leadership journey by being very clear on why we are pursuing any given project and how our project contributes value relative to other projects in the overall portfolio. With the triple constraint in mind, we recognize the importance of clarity in both product and project scope. Lack of clarity leads to waste of time, and wasted time leads to waste of budget and loss of goodwill among those contributing to our project and those waiting for our project deliverables.

We strive to turn unknown unknowns into known unknowns so that we can manage risks appropriately. We recognize that estimates carry uncertainty and seek as much expertise and past data as possible when making schedule and cost estimates. We look to the critical when looking for ways to accelerate our projects. Finally, we add the variable of earned value to our accounting analysis in order to ask the tough questions that will allow us to know if our project is within budget and on schedule.

We believe that a basic understanding of project management fundamentals is essential for anyone leading global projects. Additional resources for learning more about project management fundamentals can be accessed through the Project Management Institute (www.pmi.org) and any number of project management reference books.[2]

---

[2] For a comprehensive treatment of project management fundamentals, see "Project Management: A Systems Approach to Planning, Scheduling, and Controlling," by Harold. Kerzner, 2005, John Wiley & Sons, Inc.

Project Management Fundamentals

1. Be clear on the business strategy including corporate objectives, business unit objectives, mission statements, and vision.

2. Have a concise elevator value speech ready at all times.

3. Don't waste time. It is the most precious resource.

4. Treat key projects as you would a portfolio of investments. Understand potential value contributions and risks.

5. Clearly communicate key project milestones (deliverables and dates).

6. Clearly communicate and challenge key project assumptions. Assumptions might really be risks.

7. Understand the project constraints that limit our options for pursuing project objectives.

8. Begin detailed project planning with clear formulation of what has to be accomplished (product scope) and what has to be done (project scope) to achieve project success.

9. Scope, schedule, and budget are inextricably related to one another. Remember the triple constraint of project management.

10. Spend some extra time to turn unknown unknowns into known unknowns.

11. Focus on the critical path for time-saving opportunities.

12. Ask the tough earned value analysis questions to determine if we are within budget and on schedule.

3

The Project Story

A man walking along a dusty road came upon three bricklayers hard at work. He asked each bricklayer what he was doing. The first said, "I am laying bricks." The second man offered, "I am constructing a wall." The third bricklayer replied, "I am building a cathedral." This widely shared story of unknown origin illustrates the compelling nature of telling the project story and communicating an aspirational vision. If we walk the halls of our organization and ask people, "What are you doing?", will people be able to connect their work to something great? Are we as project leaders telling stories that inspire project team members and other stakeholders to build cathedrals rather than lay bricks? Are we involving those affected by the story in the creation of the story?

Mark Twain, in his essay titled "How to Tell a Story," said "The humorous story is American, the comic story is English, the witty story is French." There's no doubt that we approach stories differently based on personality and culture, but there are some key elements of storytelling worth considering when communicating the project story. Great stories, be they novels or project stories, have plot, characters, and conflict.

In the prologue of this book, we identified three skills of highly effective global project leaders. One is the ability to influence without authority across cultures and functions. Second, the skilled project leader is able to create project value and strategic alignment. Third, a skilled project leader is able to develop and share the project vision. This chapter on telling the project story encompasses all three skills. We share a process for creating the project story that consists of a project value elevator speech, a project vision statement, a project snapshot, and the project exit story for those times when we need to terminate a project before its planned completion. We conclude with thoughts about how to use appreciative stories to build repositories of project management best practices.

Telling the project story helps us influence others over whom we may have little or no authority. The story links our project to the value it delivers to achieving our overall strategy. Finally, our story creates purpose through a compelling vision statement. Crafting and communicating the project story may well be the most important skill required to be a highly effective global project leader.

Aspiration and Facts

We have encountered all types of project stories in our executive development work. Some leaders help us envision inspiring pictures of cathedrals while others speak the project management language of scope, work breakdown structure, milestones, and critical paths. To tell the whole project story, one that addresses the built-in conflict of competing for organizational resources and the attention of central characters while making the plot clear, we recommend a balanced approach that combines aspiration and facts. We need to know where we are going, certainly, but we also need to know why we are doing the work that we do.

As project leaders, we don't want to discover our team members in bookstores looking for books to guide them in seeking meaningful work lives. It's our job to help connect meaning to their project work. We call this the why before the what (YB4What). If someone understands why something needs to be done before we *tell* them what needs to be done, the likelihood of successful completion and the willingness to engage in future project work increases significantly. Think about your own work. How many times have you wondered why your organization is pursuing certain initiatives? Doesn't it make a difference when you are clear on the purpose?

In most organizations, project team members deal with conflicting priorities. They often have a functional boss and report dotted-line to several project managers. Most work today is filled with conflicting and competing requests vying for our attention. The E-mails at our desk and increasingly on our cell phones bombard us with mixed and often conflicting messages of how we should be spending our time. Given so many competing priorities, we as humans need to find a way to sort out why we should be working on any given project or activity versus some competing demand.

You might be surprised by how many leaders of significant projects and initiatives do not appreciate the simple connection between sense making and getting work done, YB4What. If we can't help people make sense of why they're doing something, they are likely to move on to something else. We have heard many comments like this one, "It's not my job to explain why something needs to be done.

If someone needs to be convinced that the work needs to be done, there are other places to draw a paycheck." Some of this cynicism comes from what we often see as a disconnect between corporate visions and what happens on the ground.

The project leadership story is a blending of why and what. It includes the following four elements:

1. The project value elevator speech.
2. The project vision statement.
3. The project snapshot.
4. The exit story.

Although there is certainly more to the overall project story than these elements, we differentiate between the project leadership story and the overall project management mechanisms for tracking the details of scope, schedule, budget, and other considerations such as contract administration and the like. These latter considerations cannot be overlooked, but they are often handled by institutionalized control mechanisms. We focus on the leadership components of the project story that are not typically institutionalized within an organization's project management framework.

The What–Why Dance

We cannot answer the why question until we understand what it is we want to accomplish with our project or initiative. The birth of an idea usually comes from an attempt to meet some need. We worked, for example, with a nongovernmental organization, NGO, in South Africa. This NGO provides training in psycho-social support for children afflicted in some way by HIV or AIDS. The organization was established out of the realization that children's basic food needs were being met by many organizations, but their psychological well-being and emotional needs were largely overlooked.

This NGO essentially serves as a program office from which regional training projects are monitored and supported. Our work focused largely on helping the program manager and project managers understand which projects contributed the most to their overall strategy and then communicate in the project management language deliverables, deadlines, and budgets what had to be done. Overall, the purpose, the overarching why, of the NGO was extraordinarily clear. But why they were working on any particular project was much less clear.

We visited a community of ramshackle dwellings made of scrap corrugated steel and old road signs. The community consisted largely of grandparents and children. Most of the parents had died from AIDS. During our visit to the community, we were invited to the home of a grandmother and her two granddaughters, a toddler and a 13-year-old. The toddler was HIV-positive and the 13-year-old had not yet been tested. We asked the woman where she thought the children of the community would be in 10 years. She said that most would be dead or in jail. This backdrop highlighted the enormity of the challenge facing the NGO and the urgency of the mission.

The NGO staff consisted of highly educated professionals, many of whom were psychologists or sociologists with advanced degrees. Few had any formal project management training of any type. They were accidental project managers who felt overwhelmed as a result of initiating more projects than they could ever complete. They understood that the situation with the children was desperate. The overall question of "Why?" required no debate. But they needed a clear project-by-project story to avoid burning out under the overwhelming pressure of trying to get help to as many children as possible.

Given nearly unlimited project possibilities and very limited resources, the first part of the project story focused on why any given project would deserve scarce resources potentially at the expense of not pursuing alternative projects. The first part of the project story is the value proposition, or as we explained in Chapter 2, the project value elevator speech.

Project Value Elevator Speech

Recall the motivation for a project value elevator speech. Imagine riding in an elevator with a senior leader who asks "What kind of value is your project going to deliver?" The bottom line is that if we can't identify what kind of value our project is delivering and communicate this value clearly in a concise message, we probably shouldn't be moving forward with the project. At a minimum, we had better get it straight so we can communicate why we are using scarce resources to pursue any particular project.

When the NGO project managers began formulating project value elevator speeches for their projects, they realized that some projects were more deserving of resources than others. By questioning the value of what they were doing, and how they were using their time and the time of others, they rebalanced their overall portfolio of projects. They cut the projects that didn't make sense and began using the project value elevator speech as a simple screening method for any new initiatives.

Project Story Imperative 1

Begin every project story with the project value elevator speech.

Recall James' challenge shared in Chapter 2. James was responsible for a project in which local and regional transportation and logistics providers would be replaced by a global provider. His project value elevator speech read as follows. "By consolidating with a single global third-party logistics provider, we will improve our global account management capabilities by providing global service levels and tracking capabilities. In the process, we will reduce total supply chain costs and free key leadership talent to work on revenue-generating opportunities." This concise statement addresses the central conflict of the regional approach versus the global approach. With the regional approach to logistics provision, the organization could not achieve its global account management goals. Additionally, the inefficiencies in the regional approach tied up key human resources that could otherwise be generating additional revenue. Furthermore, his elevator speech can be communicated quickly and easily.

We challenge project leaders to develop project value elevator speeches not only to be able to respond quickly to senior managers but also to demonstrate that they are bridges from strategy to implementation. Without clearly identifying the value of projects, we might complete a project within schedule and under budget without delivering any actual value. In Chapter 2, we described the process of project portfolio management as a more formal procedure for identifying individual project value and prioritizing projects within a portfolio based on risk and various forms of value such as net present value and strategic contribution. Even for organizations that have formal portfolio management systems, the importance of being able to communicate a concise statement of project value cannot be overstated.

Project value elevator speeches present clear and concise statements of value contribution. They are still more informational than aspirational. Value contribution flows from logical assumptions and even analytical approaches such as net present value calculations. The second part of the project story, the project vision statement, provides a pointer to True North. It provides the overall plot of the project story, where we are heading and what the future will look like. Before we delve into the process of developing a project vision statement, we need to address some of the shortcomings of broader organizational vision statements.

Visions from on High

We like to ask high-potential managers attending our seminars "What is your company vision?" It's a straightforward question. Can you answer this question without searching the company Intranet? If not, you are not alone. In asking this question to over a thousand participants over many years, we have found that a very small percentage can come anywhere close to reciting their company vision statements. They can capture a few key words. They can tell you where to find it. But the vision statement is clearly not guiding their everyday decision-making. If they are building cathedrals, it's not because of the vision statement.

Corporate and business unit visions paint a picture of what an organization can look like at its very best. A vision statement is, by definition, intended to be aspirational. It communicates "This is who we want to be." If the vision statement is meant to be the guiding light pointing to True North, why are the beacons of so many leadership light houses broken? Why is it that leaders who inspire us by telling compelling stories linked to the vision are the exception rather than the rule in most organizations?

We believe in the power of project vision statements. Unfortunately, in our work, we have had to overcome some of the cynicism associated with corporate vision statements. It's hard to sell anyone on the value of a project vision statement without addressing the disconnects that we see in corporate vision statements. In a nutshell, we believe that organizational vision statements tend to be developed with great intention but executed poorly or not executed at all. In Table 3.1, we outline comments that we have received from managers about their corporate vision statements.

You can probably add your own points to this list, or maybe you are fortunate to work in an organization in which a clear vision statement, communicated frequently, resonates with stakeholders and influences behaviors. By trying to appeal to all stakeholders, internal and external, an organization-wide vision statement often fails to resonate with any stakeholders. By acknowledging the shortcomings of many organizational vision statements, we can take extra care to create project vision statements that resonate with the central characters of the project story and provide a compelling glimpse of the story's conclusion. The project value elevator speech

Table 3.1 Comments about Corporate Vision Statements

1. It's too long.
2. In appealing to all stakeholders, it loses intensity for any single stakeholder group.
3. I know we have a good vision, but I don't hear senior leaders communicating it.
4. We say these great things in our vision statement, but we don't seem to act accordingly.
5. Whose vision is this? I wasn't involved in creating it.

addresses the central conflict of why we would allocate time and attention to the project. The project vision statement rallies the project stakeholders around the story's conclusion, a snapshot of the preferred future resulting from completing the project.

Creating the Project Vision Statement

We believe that project visions can be more compelling and easier to develop and manage than corporate or organization-wide vision statements. In a project-based world, we have found that describing deliverables and project work is not generally inspiring to project team members and other stakeholders. As leaders, we need to tell the project story. The story should be centered on a compelling project vision.

A project vision is a snapshot of the preferred future. Quite simply, *a project vision statement is a snapshot of the preferred future that will result from (1) achieving our project's deliverables and (2) being involved with the project as a contributor.* The vision describes what's in it for those who receive the benefits of the project deliverables and what's in it for those doing the project work. As project leaders we need to overcome the pitfalls that we tend to experience in developing and implementing organization-wide visions. We have guided many project leaders through this process and believe that certain principles backed up by simple practices can help project leaders transform their teams from bricklayers to cathedral builders.

A project leader responsible for building a factory in China attended a seminar, not one of ours, on the importance of creating a vision. He returned from the prestigious university with determination to craft a compelling vision statement. He met with a few of his trusted advisors and crafted the following statement:

The Guangzhou factory will be a world-class manufacturing facility that will produce outstanding products at the lowest possible cost. It will stand out as a benchmark admired by all in the corporation.

He shared the vision statement with the European corporate office and received glowing feedback. Encouraged by this positive feedback, the project leader decided to share the vision with the project team at a project planning meeting in Guangzhou. The core project team consisted mostly of local national manufacturing engineers and expatriate European manufacturing and industrial engineers charged with the responsibility of transferring technology from European factories to the new Chinese plant. Once constructed, the plant would be managed by a French expatriate plant manager who had plant startup experience in Mexico.

Prior to the meeting, the project leader e-mailed the project vision statement to the French plant manager who replied that the vision might be a bit of a stretch, but that it was certainly aspirational. Since it had been blessed by corporate, the plant manager did not raise any objections. The project leader approached the meeting with confidence, feeling that he had endorsement from the corporate office and the plant manager.

The presentation of the project vision statement seemed to go well. The Chinese manufacturing engineers felt excited and proud to be part of the project. The European manufacturing engineers shared, only with each other, their doubts and frustrations. Why would this new plant stand out as a benchmark? Did the Chief Executive Officer (CEO) plan to shut down European operations in favor of lower cost Chinese alternatives? In their eyes, the project vision statement suggested a strategy of moving more operations to China, and they were essentially creating the means for working themselves out of jobs.

In this example, the project vision statement resonated well with the corporate office but it did not have buy-in from some critical stakeholders, the European engineers who would be needed to transfer the technology to the Chinese plant. In their eyes, the project vision did not just fall short of being inspiring. It was threatening to the very people the project manager would depend on most to get the work done. If our vision will be used to tell a story about a desirable future, then it makes good sense to include those who will help us build the cathedral in the creation of the story.

Project Story Imperative 2

Let the project team and other key stakeholders create the project vision. We are most likely to be inspired by a vision that we create.

We have adopted an approach for developing project visions in a single highly participative exercise. Before you call for a visioning session, we recommend folding the process of developing the vision statement into a broader project planning meeting. If you send out an e-mail calling for a meeting to develop the project vision, you probably won't get the same level of attendance you would with a project planning, or project kickoff, meeting. Project people are, by definition, action oriented. The idea of coming to a visioning session can be a complete turnoff for some. We have learned this the hard way.

An ideal position for the visioning exercise is after giving the project value elevator speech to the team. Recall that the project value elevator speech goes beyond simply talking about *what* we will accomplish. The elevator value speech addresses *why* we are pursuing the project in terms of the value produced for the organization and key stakeholders. The elevator value speech is more factual than aspirational. If people were motivated by positive net present values and contributing to the strategic objectives of the organization, we probably wouldn't need project vision statements. The reality of project value, is that discussions of value contribution don't usually talk about what's in it for me (WIIFM) as an individual project contributor.

Consider the case of a major IT project at a US-based multinational. This company had five or six distinct functional "silos" each with their own IT organization that in turn had its own human resource management and finance functions, and so on. The same processes were repeated time and time again across all of these functions. The corporate Chief Information Officer (CIO) decided that the company needed to standardize some of the basic technologies and platforms and consolidate many of the support functions into a centralized shared services organization.

Once the CIO decided what she wanted to do, she had to sell the value of the project to the CEO and other key decision-makers such as the Chief Finance Officer (CFO) who had a major say in the budgeting of the project. Her elevator project value speech was quite straightforward.

> By achieving real-time visibility of sales, supply chain, financial, and human resource information on a global basis, we will strengthen our ability to increase service levels and revenues and we will decrease total supply chain costs on a percentage basis. We will also have the ability to better integrate our systems with our large global customers. This integration will allow us to pursue our global account management excellence strategy.

This elevator speech does a nice job of outlining value contribution. From this brief statement, we get a sense of customer value, tactical value, and financial value. We also see strategic value in the integration of IT systems with major global customers. However, this is not the vision. We like to think of the project value elevator speech as a stepping stone toward the project vision statement. It falls short of telling a story about a preferred future that is compelling to a broad group of stakeholders. The project value elevator speech is a bit more about what's in it for the organization. The project vision statement has to reach out to what's in it for us. As one participant in a visioning session put it, "Let's face it, if I'm reading a vision statement, I'm wondering what's in it for me."

Project Story Imperative 3

The project vision statement must include WIIFM for those who will be doing the project work as well as those who will benefit from the project deliverables.

Our process is a straightforward technique in which project team members and other key stakeholders brainstorm key words to describe the vision of a preferred future resulting from successful project completion. We are not creating something that is abstract or unrealistic. Our goal is to ask ourselves how those receiving the output of our project and those contributing to the project will benefit. The following process has proven very successful in our work with project teams.

Rapid Project Visioning Exercise

As previously stated, we recommend this exercise as part of a project kickoff meeting or a regular project planning session. Although it is ideal to create the project vision at the beginning of the project, project visions can also be very useful for creating new energy within the project team for a project that is well underway.

Should you have a large group of stakeholders, it's a good idea to form smaller groups of five or six individuals for the exercise. Create the groups such that each individual group is as diverse as possible in terms of function, level in the organization, culture, and gender. You want to include individuals who will be performing the work as well as those who will be the recipients of the project deliverables.

1. Introduce the overall purpose of the exercise. The purpose is to agree on how the project can be exciting for those involved in working toward the deliverables and those who will receive the deliverables of the project. Make it clear that we are not only developing a vision statement for the project but we are also uncovering ways to keep ourselves energized.
2. Identify the small-group team members. It's a good idea to include each of the group assignments as well as any breakout rooms, if available, on a single piece of paper to make it easy for the participants to break quickly into their groups.
3. Ask each group to spend about 15–20 minutes of individual brainstorming of key words that describe the reasons to be excited about the actual project work as well as the outcomes of the project after successfully achieving the deliverables. Each participant in the group should write down on pieces of paper their thoughts in just a few words. The aim is not

to individually craft a vision statement but rather to express as many individual ideas about the process and outcomes for the project. They should keep their thoughts separate and on separate pieces of paper that can be taped to a wall. That is, a thought about being joyful in working relationships should be separate from a thought about the customer benefits. The reason for keeping the thoughts separate is that the brainstorming process is followed by a sorting process in which themes will emerge.

4. The sorting process involves placing the individual thoughts about being involved in the project work or receiving the project deliverables into conceptual themes. If, for example, a group of 6 individuals each contributes 4 ideas for a total of 24 contributions, we typically find that the sorting process would result in no more than about 6 or 7 individual themes.

5. Ask the stakeholders to separate aspirational words from fact-based objective words. We have found that it is almost impossible to focus strictly on aspirational words and not include words that describe fact-based objectives.

6. Once we have identified themes, we can create brief sentences from the words that we see in the themes. These sentences should describe the preferred future that results from either doing the work or receiving the deliverables of the project. We can also identify a few objectives from the more fact-based words and phrases.

7. After spending some time wordsmithing sentences into a clear project vision, it's a good idea to test the project vision and objectives with additional stakeholders to ensure clarity and resonance. An effective project vision statement needs to be easy to remember and it must resonate with those doing the work and receiving the benefits of the project deliverables.

The training arm of a consulting organization initiated a project to develop online learning content that would free up critical resources needed for face-to-face client engagements. Subject matter experts (SMEs) within the organization were asked to participate in the project. They would develop tutorials and streaming video presentations. One of the senior partners believed firmly that if the organization did not embrace new technologies, it would be left behind as competitors entered the lucrative eLearning space. As he put it, "We eat their lunch or they will eat ours."

A junior partner, Alfonzo, was put in charge of this initiative. But he realized quickly that many of the SMEs had little or no time to support the initiative. They were either delivering training at client sites or they were preparing for their next client encounter. These consultants were both world-class trainers and experts in their fields. Many of them had migrated back-and-forth from industry to academia. They were clearly committed to both teaching and learning.

Schedules slipped as the SMEs were never quite available for the intensive sessions with the course designers and web developers. Finally, a senior partner, Oscar, issued an edict that made it very clear that participation was no longer optional. Over a period of a few months, several eLearning modules were developed for blended learning programs in which some eLearning would be done before and after face-to-face training.

Much to Oscar's and Alfonzo's disappointment, the rollout of the eLearning modules was a failure. From a technical standpoint, the learning technology worked well. Modules contained streaming video, flash presentations, threaded discussions, and chat capabilities. Unfortunately, the training program participants simply did not use the online modules in numbers great enough to justify the cost.

In a postmortem discussion with the client, it became clear that several problems had not been identified in advance. The capabilities of the world-class trainers did not translate into excellent online learning. The streaming video presentations were awkward at best. Additionally, the sales representatives who were the target audience for the training complained that they did not have the time to sit and listen to online computer presentations before taking the additional time to go to face-to-face training.

The SME trainers complained that they were going through the motions because the message was clear that participation was no longer optional. As one trainer put it, "I didn't get into this business to present to video cameras and moderate online discussion groups. I like Alfonzo and fear Oscar, so I stepped up to the plate. I really wish we had never moved into this eLearning space."

The consulting organization and multinational client had enough history working together that they were able to take a step back and realize that they had no real alignment around any kind of vision. The value of online learning was clear. It would reduce cost and increase the reach to salespeople around the world. What was missing was WIIFM for both the SME trainers and the recipients of the training.

A meeting was called to revisit the purpose of the training and how create the greatest buy-in and impact. The meeting included Alfonzo, Oscar, senior managers from the client organization and several of the salespeople who would be part of the target audience for the training. Alfonzo conducted a visioning exercise similar to the one we described. During the exercise, it became clear that the trainers and the recipients of the training, the salespeople, did not believe in the project. Alfonzo asked the trainers and the salespeople to go to separate breakout rooms to brainstorm responses to the following question. "If we were to do this over again, what possible benefits could you obtain from either developing the learning modules or having access to these modules?"

After some discussion, the trainers realized that they could benefit from not having to do as much basic skill-building training. Additionally, if clients would see enough value in the online learning modules, the trainers might end up getting more of the challenging custom training assignments that they enjoyed the most. The recipients of the training said they could see value in the training if the modules would be available well in advance of the face-to-face sessions and if the trainers would appear more energized in the streaming video sessions. The groups came together after their separate visioning sessions to craft the following overall vision and objectives for the project:

Project Vision: The skill-building online learning modules, delivered in a highly energetic and entertaining format, will allow us to focus on more exciting and value-added learning opportunities when we meet face-to-face.

- *Objectives*:
  - Complete the modules within 6 months.
  - Make the online modules available at least 3 weeks before any face-to-face training.
  - Obtain a satisfaction score of at least 4.3 on a five-point scale.
  - Increase our training revenue by 15% by focusing on higher-margin training and development work.

Getting the stakeholders together allowed Alfonzo the opportunity to seek alignment. The trainers understood that this was not some form of cruel punishment. In fact, they decided that more junior level SMEs could facilitate the online discussions. Additionally, the course development team worked on enhancements to streamline the online course development process. The recipients of the training understood that offloading some of the more basic material to an online format would allow for a much richer face-to-face experiences. The consulting organization agreed to post the online material several months before the face-to-face training and send periodic reminders to those who had not logged in to the modules within a few weeks of the face-to-face training.

Project Story Imperative 4

Unfreeze stalled projects by seeking WIIFM alignment through a clear vision statement supported by concise objectives.

This is not leadership wizardry. We are simply tapping into the human nature of those who need to do the work and those who will receive the output of our projects. We are building the foundations of the project story. The project vision statement is short and crisp. It resonates with those doing the project work and those receiving the benefits of the project deliverables. The project vision links to the project value elevator speech. Telling the project story is a key skill required to elevate us beyond those managing projects to leaders of projects and major initiatives. Additionally a project vision statement is supported by objectives to ensure that it is not just

Table 3.2   Project Vision Statement Leadership Checklist

- Our project vision statement provides a clear picture of the ideal project outcomes (positive impacts).
- Our project vision is positive and inspiring to project stakeholders.
- Key project stakeholders were involved in creating our project vision.
- Our project vision supports the business case (value proposition) for our project.
- Our project vision is consistent with my personal beliefs and the beliefs of my team members.
- Project team members "own" the project vision.
- Our project vision is sufficiently bold yet attainable. It doesn't reach too far beyond the limits of the project (e.g., world peace as a result of building a new production facility).
- Our project vision statement is supported by concise objectives so it does not stand alone as an unattainable dream.
- Our project vision statement is easy to remember.

a dream. The above checklist, outlined in Table 3.2, can be used when developing a project vision statement.

The Project Snapshot

The project value elevator speech and the project vision statement help to make sense of why we would work on any given project given so many conflicting demands. The project snapshot tells us how we are doing at any given point in time. It is not intended to be a substitute for comprehensive project control systems. Rather, it is a snapshot of project status and next steps.

Being able to provide a project snapshot is especially important for accidental project managers operating in an environment unsupported by formal project management. In our work with senior executives across many industries, we have been hearing terms such as PowerPoint culture to describe a tendency to provide too much information about the status of projects when summary-level information with appropriate levels of backup would suffice.

A project snapshot consists of the punch line, current status, next steps, and explanation. The general practice that we have adopted for the project snapshot is illustrated in the following example outlined

---

The punch line

With an anticipated net present value of $10 million, this project will improve the sharing of best practices across global project offices and result in increased speed and cost reductions.

Current status

We are yellow in schedule and budget and red in scope management.

Next steps

We will confirm scope requirements with the steering committee to ensure alignment of expectations and resources.

Explanation

We allowed an ad hoc process of requests from influential stakeholders to create incremental increases in project scope. Please see the appendix for a detailed listing of these requests and the impacts of these requests on schedule and budget.

Figure 3.1   A Project Snapshot.

in Figure 3.1. We advocate starting with the punch line followed by current status and next steps. Then provide any supporting explanation. This best practice has been developed from observing the reporting practices within many project-based organizations.

A great deal of dysfunction exists within organizations around project status reporting. Although senior executives tell us that they do not want 100 page PowerPoint presentations, project leaders often tell us stories of working late into the evenings preparing presentations. This clear disconnect between what senior leaders want and what project leaders think they want represents one of the great untested assumptions of most organizations. Project leaders assume more information is better. Often times this culture comes from stories of project leaders who were caught off-guard without sufficient information during a presentation to senior management. It only takes one termination after a presentation to create a culture of fear in an organization.

A project leader in an IT organization within a European company explained how he broke the culture of excessive reporting within his organization. He calculated the true costs of generating the project status presentation that often included over 150 pages of backup data. In a presentation to a senior decision board, he presented the cost of developing the presentation. The cost was in excess of €10,000. The appalled senior executives created a corporate initiative to reduce reporting requirements to the absolute core of the value-added information required to run the business. The moral of the story is to test assumptions about just how much of the project story senior executives really want to hear before consuming too many projects resources compiling lengthy presentations.

Project Story Imperative 5

Test assumptions about how much project status information is really necessary.

We have covered the basic elements of the project story including the project value elevator speech, the project vision statement, and the project snapshot. These story elements combined with more comprehensive project tracking and control systems allow us to manage and lead complex projects and initiatives. The project story aligns stakeholders around the value proposition and the highly desired future state. The project vision statement includes some aspect of WIIFM for those involved in doing the project work.

As much as we want to inspire stakeholders through a compelling vision statement and keep them on track with the project snapshot, there are times when it simply does not make sense to continue the project. When a project should not continue we need to develop the project exits story.

The Project Exit Story

Killing a project is one of the most difficult tasks for a project leader. After all, the primary goal of a project leader is to see his or her project through to successful completion. It's difficult to decouple project failure from a personal failure. However, there are many

Table 3.3 Common Reasons for Terminating Projects

- Cumulative cost increases or schedule delays can no longer be tolerated by the organization.
- The strategy for which the project was intended as changed.
- Budget cuts have forced the trimming of some projects.
- Experts have determined that the project will not meet its objectives.
- Other higher priority projects have been introduced to the project portfolio.

reasons why projects should be terminated and failure to recognize these reasons often leads to additional waste of time and talent. In Table 3.3, we have outlined some common reasons for terminating projects.

The strategy is what matters, not the project. We repeat this theme several times throughout this book. Projects represent the implementation of strategy. If the strategy changes or other projects can better support the strategy, we need to reallocate resources accordingly. Clinging to a project for the sake of personal conviction makes little sense. That said, we also hear many stories of product breakthroughs coming from projects that had been terminated at one point but kept alive by a scientist or engineer. There is no perfect formula for deciding which projects to keep and which ones to terminate, but if we display an unwillingness to terminate any project we are likely thinking in ways that are not strategic and not even in the best interest of the organization.

Telling the project exit story may actually take more courage than any other aspect of project leadership. None of us want to stand in front of a steering committee or even a single executive to explain why we should terminate our project. The project exit story is essentially the converse of the rest of the project story. We have to tell the story of why our project will not deliver value commensurate with the cost of completing the project.

We do not have an absolute template for telling the project exit story. The story will depend on which factors identified in Table 3.3, or other factors specific to your project and organization, justify termination of the project. What some project leaders fail to realize is that telling the project exit story provides an opportunity to elevate one's leadership, assuming that the reason for exit is not their own mismanagement of the project.

We are increasingly seeing project leadership as a prerequisite skill set to move into general management positions. By speaking the language of general management, we as project leaders can create strategic imperatives for reallocating resources to other projects. Project leaders who courageously tell stories of why their projects should be terminated to reallocate resources for more strategic use tend to be noticed favorably by senior management of organizations.

In addition to telling the complete project story from the project value elevator speech to, when necessary, the project exit story, we as leaders of projects and initiatives have the opportunity to *learn* from project stories. Some of the best learning comes from listening to stories.

Learning from Project Stories

Appreciative inquiry, a process and emerging field developed by David Cooperrider of Case Western Reserve University and embraced by a growing number of organizations, involves listening to stories about when things have gone really well in organizations and learning from these stories by extracting themes that describe the essence of the excellence within the organization. We have also adapted this process in working with project teams to identify what drives excellence in project work. We took the process a step further by using the story themes as the foundation for drilling deeper to determine *root causes of excellence.*

Our interest in this process was stimulated by a consulting engagement with a major automobile tire retailer. The organization wanted to improve various aspects of its services including sales and in-store customer experiences. We considered applying Six Sigma approaches to systematically define, measure, analyze, improve, and control processes. Much to our surprise and eventual delight, the client said that the problem solving focus of Six Sigma did not fit their positive culture. We stumbled upon appreciative inquiry as we looked for positive approaches to organizational improvements.

Our approach adapted from the work of many in the area of appreciative inquiry is as follows:

- Pick a topic.
- Develop and ask appreciative questions to obtain stories of excellence.
- Identify excellence themes.
- Identify root causes of excellence (the Five Hows of Excellence) for each theme.

In conducting an intervention with a project team, we used this approach to identify what drives excellence within the team when the team was functioning particularly well. Our appreciative topic was project team member effectiveness.

We asked team members to share stories that highlighted their memories of when the team was particularly effective and the roles team members had in achieving the effectiveness. We were amazed by the enthusiasm with which the project team members shared their stories. Given how positive the experience was for the team members, we began videotaping the stories. The process itself began unleashing positive energy within the team. After listening to about 50 unique stories, the following themes emerged:

- Encouraged communication.
- Identified differences and found common ground.
- Filled a leadership void.
- Influenced without formal authority.
- Demonstrated strong conviction.
- Listened skillfully.
- Demonstrated creativity.

The best way to interpret this list is to conclude that for this particular project team, these are the behaviors that contributed most to the team's effectiveness. If we were to gather stories across a random selection of teams across the entire organization, we could identify organization-wide best practices for project teams. We generally recommend the broader organizational approach since it permits individual teams to explore their own strengths and also widens the lens enough to capture best practices from across the organization.

Once we identify the themes, we can dig deeper by asking how each of the themes is achieved. We call this process the Five Hows of Excellence. It parallels the five whys approach used in root cause analysis of problems. By using a fishbone analysis, as depicted in Figure 3.2, with the excellence theme as the starting point, we can ask how we achieve the theme.

For example if the theme is "Identified differences and found common ground," the process might look like the following diagram displayed in Figure 3.3 for the branch that begins to identify

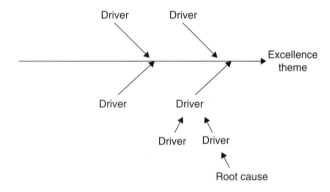

Figure 3.2   Fishbone Diagram for Root Causes of Excellence.

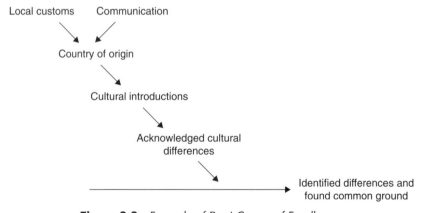

Figure 3.3   Example of Root Causes of Excellence.

specific processes for communicating cultural differences. By digging deeper than simply saying that we will acknowledge cultural differences, we uncover an approach in which project team members shared local customs and communication styles during a project kickoff meeting. When we keep asking "how?" we get to the root causes of excellence. These root causes amount to a set of specific best practices that we can use to achieve excellence in our projects.

This ability to listen to project stories and ultimately use these stories to identify specific best practices that can be used to improve current and future projects suggest that the power of stories is not only in the telling; it's also in the listening. Although one could argue that this approach is simply an internal benchmarking exercise, we have found that the positive pursuit of project excellence through stories unleashes positive energy while identifying rich sets of best practices.

Project Story Imperative 6

Listen to project stories to release positive energy while identifying best practices.

The Power of Stories

At the beginning of this chapter, we said that a good story has conflict, characters, and a plot. The project value elevator speech deals directly with the conflict inherent in all projects, the underlying conflict we experience when choosing one project over other possible projects and in deciding how to allocate energy across many projects. By clearly determining the project value, we can justify the project itself and the allocation of resources. The project vision statement captures the hearts and minds of the central characters, or key stakeholders. By involving key stakeholders in developing the project vision statement, we achieve commitment toward the benefits of participating in the project and the benefits that accrue from completing the project. The project snapshot provides a clear picture of project status with focus on the project punch line and next steps. The project exit story essentially reverses the rest of the project story. In some cases we have to depart from telling the story of why we should complete the project to explain why we should not. Finally, we concluded that we also have an obligation to listen to project stories to acknowledge positive accomplishments of team members and develop best practices that can be used in both current and future projects.

We wish you well in telling your own project stories and learning from the stories of your projects.

Project Story Imperatives

1. Begin every project story with the project value elevator speech.

2. Let the project team and other key stakeholders create the project vision. We are most likely to be inspired by a vision that we create.

3. The project vision statement must include WIIFM for those who will be doing the project work as well as those who will benefit from the project deliverables.

4. Unfreeze stalled projects by seeking WIIFM alignment through a clear vision statement supported by concise objectives.

5. Test assumptions about how much project status information is really necessary.

6. Listen to project stories to release positive energy while identifying best practices.

Cross-Cultural and Cross-Functional Project Leadership Skills

All things considered, there are only a two kinds of men in the world – those who stay at home and those who do not. The second are the more interesting.
Rudyard Kipling, In the Honorable Visitors

Guus Hiddink, an excellent leader of global projects, is probably a pretty interesting person. Many readers may not recognize his name. But why is he an excellent leader of global projects and an interesting person? What did he accomplish? What skills does he have in working across cultures?

We will shortly provide some clues.

In Chapter 4, we are providing space for readers to respond to a few questions. It is not necessary to write in the space and there are no right or wrong answers. We do expect you will think about the answers to the questions we ask.

We begin this chapter with some questions. They are questions outside the professional responsibilities of leaders of global projects but we suspect that many would have the correct answers.

The first question is easy. What is the world's most popular sport? Okay you could say what does popular mean? We mean popular in the sense of what is the world's most played/watched sport by more people than any other. If you said football or soccer you would be correct. The world's most popular sport is football.

Here's another question that is a little more difficult. In the year 2002, where was the World Cup held? The World Cup is held every 4 years and it is when the best teams in the world compete for the championship of football. If you answered Korea and Japan you answered correctly.

Next question. In the year 2002 who won the World Cup? The correct answer is Brazil. Who did they beat? Correct answer is Germany.

How well did South Korea do? Most people do not know the answer to this question. In the year 2002 South Korea made it to the semifinals of the World Cup. They were fourth in the world.

The Korean national soccer team had never won a World Cup game prior to 2002 since they first qualified for the World Cup in 1954. Why were the Koreans so successful in the year 2002?

The success of the 2002 World Cup is deeply experienced by most Koreans and will probably be remembered in Korean history for a long time as the coach of the South Korean team at that time was a Dutch person whose name is Guus Hiddink. Hiddink is credited with being the person most responsible for the success of the Korean national team.

The Dutch coach was a leader of a global project...and an interesting person. The scope of his project was to win matches in the World Cup. His task was global; he was Dutch all players were Korean. Figure 4.1 shows a picture of coach Hiddink.

What the Dutch coach observed was the following. First there was a significant lack of open communication between the players on the Korean national soccer team. The youngest player on the team, Mr. Park, age 20, was playing a position that required him to communicate freely and quickly with all the other players

Figure 4.1   Soccer Coach's Dilemma.

on the field. However as the youngest player on the team he was having difficulty speaking to the older players on the team and he was expected to use the proper "honorifics" when speaking with the older players.

Another problem that Mr. Park experienced, was that he was the subject of constant criticism from the senior players if he made any mistakes. In the world-class teams in Europe and other countries players are praised by their teammates but on the Korean national team there were very few positive reinforcements. Instead many of the young Korean players were concerned about the criticism they would receive from their more senior players if they made any mistakes or did not score when they had a good opportunity.

The Dutch coach also noticed that the younger players often took the blame for a more senior player when a mistake was made regardless of who was really at fault.

Another problem and perhaps a more serious one, was that the younger players tended to pass to the more senior players when there was the possibility of scoring. This became a serious problem as the other teams would notice this pattern and would double-team the more senior players or anticipate a pass to this person as it became predictable.

What did Hiddink do? As team leader he did several things. First he required all of the players to eat their meals with players from different age groups. With the help of Korean "cultural interpreters"

Hiddink determined that the only way they would break the "cultural patterns" identified previously, which were perhaps hundreds or thousands of years old in Korean society, was if the more senior players on the team gave permission for the more junior players on the team, when they were playing soccer. Then they could break the pattern of giving deference to the most senior players and pass to whoever was in the best position to score.

This resulted in a kind of group dynamic that was exceedingly powerful and had a significant positive result namely in the year 2002 in the World Cup of soccer the South Korean national team made it to the semifinals. WOW.

This is an example of a skillful leader of a global project.

A Newspaper Column

Now let us turn to an example which is not quite so exemplary. Ann Landers, before she died was a widely read American syndicated columnist. Her columns which covered topics of relationships between husbands and wives, children and their parents as well as many other human relationships subjects appeared in hundreds of newspapers around the world.

One column concerned a Vietnamese Canadian living in Vancouver Canada. In the Vietnamese Canadian's letter to Ann Landers she stated she came from a very large, middle-class Asian family who emigrated from Vietnam 10 years ago. The letter went on to say that her family was treating her "like a child." She said she was an "obedient and dutiful daughter; a straight A student but she was not allowed to go out on any dates even though she is more than 20-years old." She also stated that she needed her mother's "permission to do most things." She ended her published letter by saying she is a loner and that many other Asian children are in the same position. She signed her letter "Repressed and Oppressed."

Ann Landers answered as follows. "With all due respect to your cultural heritage, a woman of 22 should be free to have friends both male and female, so that she can develop culturally and emotionally as well as intellectually. I urge you to discuss this problem with a professor at your school. Your mother's life has been a very hard-won and she deserves respect, but you are entitled to a life of your own and I urge you to assert yourself."

We had the opportunity to show the original letter written by the Vietnamese young woman living in Canada and Ann Lander's response to a number of Vietnamese Americans working in the United States. We asked them how sophisticated and appropriate was her response? If they were teachers or professors, what grade would they give Ms. Landers? Would they give her an A, which is excellent, a B, a C, which is average, or a D or F, which is a failure? We spent some time discussing the situation with these Vietnamese. They fairly quickly agreed and said if they were teachers they would give Ann Landers the grade of D. When we asked why, they said because her response was almost 100% through American or Western eyes, and she didn't understand the dilemma at all posed by this young woman. We then ask them if how they would improve the grade? How could the grade change from a D to an A? This required more discussions and here's what they concluded. They said the following. The first sentence would be something like this. "You were born in Vietnam where you were socialized with Vietnamese/Asian values but now you're living in Canada where there are some differences. Finding the balance is difficult and will take time." That first sentence would have communicated to the young woman and to the millions of readers of this column when you come from one country to another it is impossible to leave behind your culture. And it is also a bad idea because you may bring something that others can learn from.

The next sentence would be something like this. "In the community in Vancouver there are people known and respected by your mother, Vietnamese who have come to Canada and have successfully adapted/integrated into the Canadian culture. These individuals have the possibility of influencing your mother." The professor is not a good solution because in Asia personal family problems are not solved outside of the family system.

Cultural Filters

Why did Ann Landers respond the way she did? Why was her answer, at least in the opinion of most people who read the response so completely Western? Why did her answer not take into account the culture, the background or the DNA of the young Vietnamese Canadian who wrote to her? And why do leaders of global projects and global teams often look at the issues and challenges in the project only through their own "lens?"

The answer can be illustrated by a story that we tell in our seminars. It is a "going to the dentist" story. Most people do not look forward to visiting their dentist, unless they have major pain. Many years ago, one of us had a dental appointment, arrived a little early, and was greeted by the receptionist and asked to wait a few minutes as the dentist was seeing another patient. A few minutes later, the dentist was ready and invited the person to sit in the dental chair. After some brief pleasantries the dentist said, "Open up wide and let me check to see how you are doing."

After participants in our program have listened to this story, we ask them two questions. "Please raise your hand if you thought the receptionist was a woman?" Most, but not all, raise their hands. "Raise your hand if you thought the dentist was a man." Most, but not all, raise their hands.

Then we tell them the reality. In fact, the receptionist was a man and the dentist was a woman. This illustrates that we "see" things from our own perspective and experience and our "cultural filters" block out important information and perspectives.

Leaders of global projects need to develop the skill of looking at important projects/issues through "multiple lens" not just their own lens. Leaders need to understand their projects and how the members of their team "see" the issues. Ann Landers' response showed she looked at the issue presented by the Vietnamese woman without considering the family of the young woman. The suggestion to go out and "assert yourself" would probably not work. But if the person was American or Canadian, it may have been rated a higher grade by the Vietnamese who read the column.

Stereotypes

We all have stereotypes or categories or classifications that help organize information. The word itself did not occur in the English language until 1922 when Walter Lippmann first used it in his book *Public Opinion*. He said that stereotypes, "Organize images, are fixed and simplified, contain certain features that are chosen to stand for the whole."

Lippmann also believed that stereotypes are essentially incorrect, inaccurate, and therefore undesirable. Other researchers and writers believe that a person's stereotypes "may contain an element of truth."

We believe that all leaders of global projects have stereotypes. We also believe they serve a purpose in reducing ambiguities. The DANGER IS THAT MOST STEREOTYPES ARE PARTIALLY ERRONEOUS. Determining the *degree* that any stereotype held by a person is "true" or "false" is difficult.

Here is an example. Through many "eyes" and in many different ways, we are told about Egypt. What you think about Egypt and Egyptians, that is, the stereotype we have determines to a large extent how you feel about traveling to Egypt, where you will go and what you expect the Egyptians to be like. When we visit Egypt what we perceive will be largely determined by our stereotypes.

Lippmann wrote:

> ...the accounts of returning travelers are often an interesting tale of what the traveler carried abroad with him on his trip. If he carried chiefly his appetite, a zeal for tiled bathrooms, and a belief that it is proper to tip waiters, taxicab drivers and barbers, but under no circumstances ushers, then his odyssey will be replete with good meals and bad meals, and voracious demands for money.

In Figure 4.2 he presents some of the factors that might influence a leader's perception of members of a global project team that often result in stereotypes of a people.

Margaret Mead the great cultural anthropologist said that she prepared for her travels not by learning languages or reading what other people have written about a culture or people. Instead she found her most important preparation is understanding HERSELF.

Past travel to that country	Degree of contact with persons from that country	Opinions of people who have visited that country	Opinion of "expert"
Economic and political news from the country	**Stereotypes of a country or people**		General past travel experience
	Products from that country	History that is known about the country	

Figure 4.2   Stereotypes of a Country or People.

She learned that to know about ones' self is the secret to beginning to learn about others. Her advice was simply to get our own "humanity" into proper focus.

The following is a list of stereotypes. The source is unknown but it may result in some smiles. A global project team should have:

> The precision of an Italian
> The generosity of a Dutchman
> The humility of a Frenchman
> The charm of a German
> The linguistic ability of an American
> The ready wit of a Scandinavian
> The internationalism of an Englishman
> The diplomacy of an Israeli
> The culture of an Australian
> The gaiety of a Swiss
> The road manners of a Belgian
>
> *Source*: Unknown.

All are stereotypes, n'est-ce pas.

Global Leaders as Learners

The challenges of skillfully working as a leader of global projects across cultures and across functions are many. Skillful leaders are also learners and benefit from their mistakes. Please read the descriptions of the following different mini-cases involving communications/interactions between leaders of global projects from different cultures and/or functions. There is no "road map" to successfully communicate in cross-functional, cross-cultural and matrix settings, but there are "road-mapping skills" that highly increase the possibilities to succeed.

These mini-cases were written and used in a leading global projects program and are used with the permission of the persons sharing the situation. Each situation is described, a question to consider is provided, followed by an alternative suggestion for readers to consider.

Mini-Case One: Responding to an e-mail?

An e-mail from a New Boss

Only a few days after Michael, a European, had arrived in Japan he was reading and replying to e-mails received from his new Japanese colleagues. He was willing to support them as much as possible, and was very interested in being accepted by the new organization as the new boss. He, therefore, carefully worded his e-mail replies. He also tried to provide advice and guidance whenever he felt it could be useful for his Japanese colleagues as he was their new boss.

One e-mail he had received had important documents attached and had been widely distributed to his colleagues. Unfortunately, the draft had not been shared with Michael prior to distribution. Both the mail text and the document had been prepared very carefully by his Japanese colleagues and the content was almost 100% perfect. Overall, he was very pleased.

However, he decided that he should provide some suggestions to the Japanese authors. He wanted to ensure that in the future, he would have the chance to review such important documents before they are sent out. So he added his reply:

"… The documentation you had put together and sent out was very well done. I thank you very much for your hard work and would kindly ask you to consider my above thoughts when preparing these kinds of documents. Perhaps in the future, you can share the draft version with me prior to sending it out : -)
Best Regards,
Michael"

After his Japanese colleagues had received his reply, they immediately got together to discuss corrective actions as they felt very committed to meeting all the expectations of their new boss. Thinking he was very angry, they tried to find out what went wrong on their side, how to then reply to their boss, and how to establish a special review process. But even after longer discussions, they found no serious mistakes and everybody was unsure about how to proceed.

What was Michael's mistake? What was the Japanese error?

_____

_____

_____

_____

_____

_____

Mini-Case One: Responding to an e-mail – Alternative

At this point, another new expatriate, Tom, came to the meeting room and they decided to approach him for advice. Tom looked briefly at the mail from Michael and then said, "Don't worry too much, no immediate action needed. Michael is very happy; just keep in the loop a bit earlier." Everybody asked Tom, "How do you know?" Tom replied, "Well, just look at the smiley he sent to you at the end of the mail text!"

None of the Japanese colleagues were familiar with the icons used in electronic communications in the western world. To express a message similar to : -) in Japan, one would use \ ^_^ /

Now everyone was smiling.

Other alternatives?

_____

_____

_____

_____

_____

_____

Mini-Case Two: German/Japanese Direct Negotiations

"Our legal person – she is a very intelligent person and an excellent negotiator. She was born in Germany but has spent many years in the United States and Canada. One would think she was an

American by the way she presents herself and by her accent. During negotiations, I have noticed that she would speak very fast with never ending sentences. Even I would get lost in her message. I can only imagine what the Japanese thought. I could get a sense that they were not following and getting a bit frustrated. Also, the lawyer would not be patient. She would not let them reiterate or make a comment but rather try to say the same thing in another way…"

The attorney's style of communication didn't seem to work.

Why?

_____

_____

_____

_____

_____

_____

_____

Mini Case Two: German/Japanese Direct Negotiations – Alternative

An American also in attendance gave Katrin, the attorney, the following feedback.

1. Speak slowly, using shorter sentences. Listen before going on to a new topic.
2. Let the Japanese respond to questions before continuing.
3. Be patient.
4. Listen. We may be hurting our own negotiations by not listening. The fact that you would not let them reply may cause us to lose out on a good situation or option.
5. To further help the Japanese understand, project your points on a screen and include the written agreement typing changes on the screen to help the discussions. That way, everyone can read and hear what you are trying to say.

Lesson

Have the courage to give feedback to senior persons.
  Have the humility to listen to feedback and to learn.

Other alternatives?

_____

_____

_____

_____

_____

_____

Mini-Case Three: Giving/Receiving Feedback on Project Teams

Barbara is an American and earned a Ph.D. in chemistry and has worked for Dieter, A Swiss, for approximately 6 months. Their working relationship is good and both are very skilled professionals. Dieter also has a Ph.D. in chemistry. Barbara is frustrated with Dieter because he has never given her any positive feedback on her work. The only time any feedback was offered was when Barbara made a rare mistake, and in this case the feedback was negative and strong.

What would you do if you were Barbara? Dieter?

_____

_____

_____

_____

_____

_____

Mini-Case Three: Giving/Receiving Feedback on Project Teams – Alternative

Americans who work together are observed giving positive feedback to their co-workers on a regular basis. Europeans tend to give less positive feedback, and this tradition is also rooted in most European education systems.

Barbara and Dieter probably need to adjust both their expectations and styles as they work together – Barbara by not expecting many positives from Dieter but trying to get it from somebody else. Dieter by respecting and understanding the need for positive feedback as a great motivator for some people and therefore a potentially important factor for project success.

Other alternatives?

_____

_____

_____

_____

_____

_____

Mini-Case Four: A Common Vision Across Functions

Michael, an American, has had considerable experience in participating and leading projects within a marketing function for a small pharmaceutical company. He has a bachelor's degree in biology and an MBA from the University of Michigan. As part of the curriculum, he took a project management class where all technical aspects of project management were at least covered.

He has been given increasing project management responsibilities and found his biggest hurdles were working across functions in a matrix organization. He had difficulty in "creating a common vision that united the various functions." Too many people seemed to be "doing their own thing." Michael did not know what to do.

What would you do if you were Michael?

_____

_____

_____

_____

_____

_____

Mini-Case Four: A Common Vision Across Functions – Alternative

To successfully lead global projects across functions, particularly in a matrix organization, it is critical to understand each other's objectives. Project leaders must not only participate in developing a common vision for the project team, but also for the stakeholders and be able to "sell" it (meaning the benefit) to all functions and divisions. To accomplish this, key individuals from all functions must:

1. Participate in the development to the vision,
2. Have a thorough understanding of the benefits and how the project supports their functional objectives and functional synergy.

In addition, the project leader must:

1. Be able to understand how the project supports each of the players,
2. Adopt the communication and presentation of potential risks, benefits and project value to each stakeholder.

This requires up-front time and has to be prepared and planned thoroughly. When the commitment and "common vision" is established, the project development can be executed much faster and with fewer hurdles.

Mini-Case Five: A Hurt Medical Director

Di has had considerable experience in participating and leading projects within a marketing department. She has been lately
working on a very challenging regional workshop involving different countries and different functions. As part of this workshop,
Di has to develop the scientific program involving regional and
international speakers and therefore she has to work very closely
with her local product manager, Theresa, as well as fully involve
her medical director, TB, with whom she usually interacts on a
daily basis.

To start working on the project, Di sent the following e-mail to
different people working in different functions: to Assad, Mariam
and David in sales, to Theresa in marketing and to TB in medical.

Dear All,
We need to start working on the logistics of the event ASAP. Mariam/
David can you please send us the list of your customers by Wednesday
evening. Let us all meet on Thursday in the office for a brainstorm session
to finalize those names. Then we need to proceed ASAP with the visas.
Mariam, plz coordinate with our agent about the visas. We have
applications in the office and he will tell you what are the papers
needed. I have already spoken to him. Assad, I need your support with
our travel agent for the tickets. The best option will be Lufthansa. I
asked them since last week for an offer and yet did not get anything
we cannot wait longer. Can you please ask them to book tentatively
for 50 delegates from 15–18 June. In the meantime, I am working with
Theresa on the scientific program and on the social program which
should be finalized by the end of this week.
Please let me know if I missed anything.
Best regards.
Di

The following day Di receives a phone call from the medical
director who was very much annoyed from her communication
because it did not include the medical department and its role in
preparing the event.

Did Di make a mistake?

_____

_____

_____

_____

_____

_____

Mini-Case Five: A Hurt Medical Director – Alternative

Di was puzzled from his call as for her it was a fact that medical will be involved in the preparation of the event because she always prepares the scientific program with the medical director.

At a later stage, the medical director explained to her that he was frustrated because whoever will read this communication would feel as if the medical department was not involved and this will undermine the efforts of the medical director to portray the medical department as an equal partner in the business and that is why it was important to state this in the communication, despite the fact that this agenda is always worked with the medical director.

Other alternatives?

_____

_____

_____

_____

_____

_____

A Framework

Culture is a distinctly human means of adapting to circumstances and transmitting this coping skill and knowledge to subsequent generations. Culture gives people a sense of who they are, of belonging, of

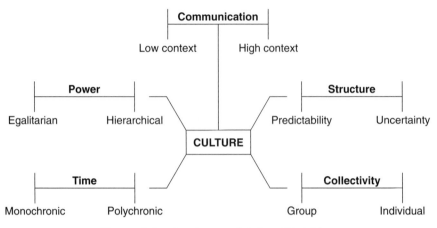

Figure 4.3   Continuum of Cultural Variables.

how they should behave, and of what they should be doing. Culture impacts behavior, morale, and productivity at work, and includes values and patterns that influence company attitudes and actions.

Culture is often considered the driving force behind human behavior everywhere. However most of what culture comprises of exists far below the surface. It is as if culture were an iceberg, and what we can "see" is only the small portion that rises above the water. Far more exist below the surface.

The above "framework" in Figure 4.3 for understanding deeper aspects of culture will be useful in analyzing "the mini-cases" of cultural misunderstanding and learning for leaders of global projects.

The following is a list tips for working with:

Low Context Cultures	High Context Cultures
Be quick, to the point, and efficient	Remember that there are many ways to get things done
Be prepared for rational, professional arguments, and presentations that push for agreements	Respect a person's title, age, background connections – whatever issue is being discussed

Predictability-Oriented Cultures	Uncertainty-Tolerant Cultures
Be specific and precise in communication	Be prepared for vagueness in communication
Drive for specific conclusions	Recognize that it may take longer to make decisions

Monochronic Cultures	Polychronic Cultures
Do one activity at a time	Do more than one activity at a time
Keep appointments strictly, schedule in advance, do not run late	Believe appointments are approximate and subject to giving time to others
Relationships are generally subordinate to schedules	Schedules are generally subordinate to relationships
Have a strong preference for following initial plans	Have strong preference for following where relationships lead

Group Focused Cultures	Individual Focused Cultures
Show patience for time taken to consent and to consult	Prepare for quick decisions
Negotiators agree tentatively, then consult with superiors	Negotiators can make commitments
The aim is to build lasting relationships	The aim is to make a quick deal
It is more important to "maintain" your relationship	It is more important to "win your objective"

Equalitarian Cultures	Hierarchical Cultures
Respect your knowledge and information of your counterparts even if you suspect they are short of influence back home	Respect the status and influence of your counterparts, even if you suspect they are short of knowledge. Do not show them up
Use the title that reflects how competent you are as an individual	Use the title that reflects your degree of influence in the organization

A Great Project Leadership Story

One of the greatest leadership stories of the last century is the story of the great Antarctic explorer Ernest Shackleton. He is credited as one of the "best leaders ever" for saving the lives of his 27 member crew who were stranded on an ice flow in the Antarctic for almost 2 years. The original scope of his project was to be the first to walk across Antarctica. A few years earlier Shackleton attempted to be the first to reach the South Pole. He did not succeed. The map in Figure 4.4 will help you understand his journey. His ship was named Endurance.

In the best leadership book we have ever read, *Shackleton's Way: Leadership Lessons From the Great Antarctic Explorer*. The authors Morrell and Capparell analyze the diaries of Shackleton and the crew and asked how did Shackleton lead, what did he do? Leadership is not theoretical – leadership is behavior.

The following are behaviors Morrell and Capparell identified that we believe are particularly relevant to leaders of global projects.

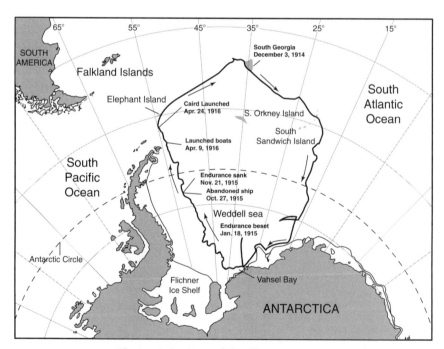

Figure 4.4   Map of Shackleton's Journey

Shackleton's Way of Developing Leadership Skills
- Broaden your cultural and social horizons beyond your usual experiences.
- Find a way to turn setbacks and failures to advantage.
- Be bold in vision and careful in planning.
- Never insist on reaching a goal at any cost.

Shackleton's Way of Selecting and Organizing a Crew
- Start with a solid core of talent you know from past experience.
- Your No. 2 is your most important person.
- Work with those who share your vision.
- Be a creative, unconventional interviewer if you seek creative, unconventional people.
- Surround yourself with cheerful, optimistic people.
- Hire those with the talents and expertise you lack.

Shackleton's Way of Forging a United and Loyal Team
- Always keep the door open to all.
- Where possible, have people work together on certain tasks.
- Be fair and impartial.
- Lead by example.
- Have regular meetings to build spirit de corps.

Shackleton's Way of Developing Individual Talent
- Be generous with programs that promote the well being of your staff. Healthy bodies and minds are more productive.
- Make sure each person has challenging and important work.
- Match the person to the position.
- Give consistent feedback on performance.
- Strive for work relationships that have a human as well as professional element.
- Reward the individual as well as the group.

Shackleton's Way of Getting the Group Through a Crisis
- Get rid of unnecessary middle layers of authority.
- Plan several options in detail.

- Keep your malcontents close to you.
- Ask for advice and information from a variety of sources.

Shackleton's Way of Forming Groups for the Toughest Tasks
- The best way to handle the biggest tasks is often to divide the staff into teams.
- Make sure you have some highly skilled individuals who can handle tough challenges.
- Empower the team leaders so they have the authority to handle their own team.
- Do not be afraid to change your mind when you see your plan is not working.

Shackleton's Way of Finding the Determination to Move Forward
- Go-for-broke risks become more acceptable as options narrow.
- Seek inspiration in enduring wisdom that has comforted or motivated you or others in times of crisis.
- Congratulate yourself and others for a job well done.
- Let your team inspire you.

Framing the Problem

Globalization is an increasingly controversial topic. In reality, the globalization roots began centuries ago when courageous explorers funded by European kings and queens sought new trade routes and the riches in the East. During the last century the level of global trade increased dramatically most years. Thomas Friedman, in his book characterized the world today as "flat" and the "playing field" is "flattening" and most peoples are taking part or being influenced by globalization.

In the arena of global successes, there are many examples such as the IKEA group the world's largest furniture group or Shiseido the world's fourth largest cosmetics company who has been in China since 1981, or Li and Fung Inc. a Hong Kong based company that connects hundreds of factories in Asia and India with large customers in Europe and the United States or Procter and Gamble, a US based company and one of the largest in the world.

There are also many examples of global failures such as Daimler Chrysler or Euro Disney at least in the initial years of construction and operations in France.

On a smaller scale, over the years, we have heard many examples of global projects that are successes or failures. The reasons for failure are many but the words of Ed Schein succinctly say much.

> *Consider any complex, potentially volatile issue—Arab relations, the problems between Serbs, Croats, and Bosnians, corporate decision making, getting control of the US deficit or healthcare costs, labor/management relations, and so on. At the root of the issue we are likely to find communication failures and cultural misunderstandings that prevent the parties from framing the problem in a common way, and thus make it impossible to deal with the problem constructively.*

We think the key words are "framing the problem in a common way." When we have applied these words to leaders of global projects, many have agreed. They have examples of scope that are not being framed in a common way, changes in schedule are not framed in a common way and problems and misunderstandings persist because strategies are not commonly understood and failing projects are not killed because the realities are denied or not framed so the stakeholders understand the consequences.

In the geopolitical, we recently read of an exchange between an American and a Vietnamese concerning the Vietnam War that ended over 30 years ago. This example illustrates the necessity to "frame problems in a common way." The dialogue is cited in Robert McNamara's book, *Argument Without End*. We have italicized the key sentences.

> *Colonel Quach Hai Luong: I want to as you: What do you think the American objectives were in Vietnam?*
>
> *Colonel Herbert Schandler: Our objectives in Vietnam, as stated by our various presidents, were the following. First, to establish and independent, noncommunist South Vietnam whose people had the ability to choose their own leaders and form of government. A second objective was to convince North Vietnam—not to defeat or crush or obliterate North Vietnam—but to*

convince North Vietnam not to impose its will on the South by means of military force. We had no burning desire even to harm North Vietnam in any way. We just wanted to demonstrate to you that you could not win militarily in the South.

Colonel Quach Hai Luong: But Colonel Schandler, if I may say so, this was a critical difference between your understanding of the situation and our understanding of it. Let me put it this way: your fundamental assumption is that Vietnam was two distinct—two rightfully independent – countries. On that basis, your objectives and strategies follow. We did not make that distinction. We saw only one country. All our strategies were based on this basic premise: that Vietnam is one country, unfortunately and artificially divided in two. Our war was for the purpose of protecting our independence and maintaining our national unity.

Leaders Handling Two Swords at the Same Time

The leaders of global projects need significant skills. In some ways, this person needs to adapt her/his leadership behavior depending on the culture of the people she/he is leading. The skillful leader must do what Miyamoto Musashi, a famous 17th-century Japan samurai, did. He developed the Nitoryu style of swordsmanship, or the act of handling two swords at the same time.

To be skillful, effective, and successful in one's own culture by being assertive, quick, and to the point is one mode of behavior. To be equally successful in another culture by being unassertive, patient, and somewhat indirect is another mode entirely – like handling two swords at the same time internationally.

Here is another exercise to illustrate what we mean. Read the adjectives and circle the ones that you believe apply to you.

Assertive, energetic, decisive, ambitious, confident, aggressive, quick, competitive, impatient, impulsive, quick-tempered, intelligent, excitable, informal, versatile, persuasive, imaginative, original, witty, colorful, calm, easy-going, good-natured, tactful, unemotional, good listener, inhibited, shy, absent-minded, cautious, methodical, timid, lazy, procrastinator, like responsibility, resourceful, individualist, broad interests, limited interest, good team-worker, like to work alone, sociable, cooperative, quiet, easily distracted, serious, idealistic, ethnocentric, cynical, conscientious, flexible, mature, dependable, honest, sincere, reliable, loyal adaptable, curious.

The next step in the exercise is to think of the scientists, technicians, lawyers, and others who are on your global project. Ask yourself in what culture were they raised, or what is their DNA? Now go back to the same list of words and place a check beside those qualities that you believe these persons will look for in you. Our hunch is there are a number of differences.

We all have our basic personality characteristics, the sword that made us successful – aggressiveness, competitiveness for example. In another culture, the second sword we are expected to carry might be characterized by qualities such as gentleness, cooperativeness, indirectness, and commitment to relationships.

Effective leaders have learned that some of their strengths if carried to the extreme become liabilities. They have also learned some of these qualities are not strengths in different cultures, have learned to "carry two swords at the same time."

The English Language as the Language of Business

For the past many years, the dominant language of international business has been English. This trend is continuing whether it is Americans talking with Japanese or Japanese with Germans or Germans with Saudi Arabians or Saudi Arabians with Brazilians.

For leaders of global projects here are some "tips" when using English. These tips apply primarily to native English speakers or when English is used as a second language of business.

- Restrict your use of English words to their most common meaning.
- Select a word with few alternate meanings (e.g., "accurate" – 1 meaning) rather than a word with many alternate meanings (e.g., "right" – 27 meanings).

- Become aware of words whose primary meaning is restricted in some cultures. For example, outside of the United States, "check" most commonly means a financial instrument and is frequently spelled "cheque."
- Become aware of alternate spellings of commonly used words and the regions in which those spellings are used: for example, colour/color, organisation/organization, centre/center.
- Conform to basic grammar rules more strictly than is common in everyday conversation. Make sure that sentences express a complete thought.
- Avoid "word pictures," constructions that depend on invoking a particular mental image (e.g., "run that by me," "wade through these figures," "slice of the free world pie").
- Avoid terms borrowed from sports (e.g., "struck out," "field that question," "touchdown," "can't get to first base," "ballpark figure"), the military, (e.g., "run it up the flag pole," "run a tight ship"), or literature (e.g., "catch-22").
- When writing to someone you do not know well, use their last name and keep the tone formal while expressing personal interest or concern.

Besides these points, we recommend the following:

1. Oral presentations should be made plainly, clearly, and slowly, using visual aids whenever possible.
2. Paraphrase in intercultural conversations, encouraging your counterpart to do the same with your input.
3. Important international business communications by telephone should be confirmed by e-mail.
4. International meetings should be facilitated with a written summary.
5. Do not tell jokes. Jokes rarely translate well since the premise is often language-specific. On the other hand, it is not necessary to eliminate humor from meetings. A humorous remark about a project or situation that is easily understood by all team members can contribute to a relaxed, productive atmosphere.

Examples of Humor

Here are some signs written in English by non-native speakers of English. Before our conclusion, we present these in hopes some may make you smile (whether you are a native English speaker or a non-native speaker).

- *In a Bucharest hotel lobby*: The lift is being fixed for the next day. During that time we regret that you will be unbearable.
- *In a Paris hotel elevator*: Please leave your values at the front desk.
- *In a Japanese hotel*: You are invited to take advantage of the chambermaid.
- *On the menu of a Swiss restaurant*: Our wines leave you nothing to hope for.
- *In a Hong Kong supermarket*: For your convenience, we recommend courteous, efficient self-service.
- *In an East African newspaper*: A new swimming pool is rapidly taking shape since the contractors have thrown in the bulk of their workers.
- *In an advertisement by a Hong Kong dentist*: Teeth extracted by the latest methodists.
- *At a Budapest zoo*: Please do not feed the animals. If you have any suitable food, give it to the guard on duty.
- *In the office of a Roman doctor*: Specialist in women and other diseases.   *Source*: Unknown

Summary Check List

Leaders of global projects are like a conductor of an orchestra. This is a check list to determine if you have the skills to conduct the "orchestra" of your project.

1. Identify the three or four leadership qualities that are most relevant for you in the project you are leading at this time.
   -
   -
   -
   -

2. Now rate yourself as possessing these qualities:
   - A little_____
   - Somewhat_____
   - A lot_____

3. Consider a global project you are working on now. List the most important skills that will influence the success of the project. Do you have individuals on your team with these prerequisite skills?

Skill	Person to Perform
_____	_____
_____	_____
_____	_____
_____	_____
_____	_____
_____	_____
_____	_____

4. A team's productivity, satisfaction and trust are a function of the *talent* on the team, minus losses due to faults or problems in how the team works together. The following is a listing of potential faults or problems. Check the ones that apply to your project.

	Does Not Apply	Applies	Action
Hidden Agenda	_____	_____	_____
Unclear Objectives/ Goals	_____	_____	_____
Stereotyping Others	_____	_____	_____
Language/ Communication Barriers	_____	_____	_____

Unclear Decision-Making Process	_____	_____	_____
Dominant/Timid Cultures and Personalities	_____	_____	_____
Clear Timeline Is Set	_____	_____	_____
Unclear Leadership Roles	_____	_____	_____
Poor Leadership	_____	_____	_____
Trust Not Established	_____	_____	_____

5. The project leader is a kind of psychologist. Human behavior is all we see. Why do we behave the way we do? Because of:
   - Our culture
   - Our personality
   - Our context

Are you, as a project leader, an astute observer of the meaning of the behavior of your team members or do you "miss" important signals?

5

Influencing and Negotiating

> *The most skillful project leaders have perfected the skill of being comfortable while being uncomfortable.*

> *Fast, cheap, good—you can have any two.*

We often ask participants in our leading global projects seminars this question, "What are the most important challenges you experience in your role as a leader of global projects?" The following are consistently mentioned.

- How can I better understand global counterparts and communicate effectively across cultures?
- How can I get real support from the steering committee?
- How can I motivate individuals to be enthusiastic about the project?
- What approaches can I use to influence others in a matrix organization when I am dealing with different cultures and functions and have little or no authority over those whom I am trying to influence?

By far, the greatest challenge is the latter – influencing across functions and cultures. Our answer to this influencing question is as follows. First, we must understand how power and influence can be used effectively by leaders of global projects. Second, most project leaders would benefit from further developing and enhancing their negotiation skills, and related ability to deal with conflict, since an important component of influence without authority is negotiating and mediating conflict.

Before we delve into influencing, negotiating, and dealing with conflict, we need to be clear on just what we mean by influence and how it differs from persuasion or manipulation. Manipulation is the dark side of influence or persuasion. We can use skillful persuasion and influencing tactics, but if we are manipulating we are by definition creating an unfair advantage. Taken to an extreme, the use of formal authority can easily cross the line into the realm of manipulation. Persuasion and influencing are highly related, but it is important to understand the subtle differences. Persuasion involves enticing someone into action largely through logic and reason. Influencing takes one further step in that those we are influencing feel a compelling force to take certain actions or behave in particular ways. In other words, I can persuade you to do some work on my project, perhaps by laying out the logic, but you may feel more cajoled than compelled.

Influencing is more than making a persuasive speech. It involves truly understanding the world of the person being influenced and what that person really wants and needs, and then fulfilling those wants and needs. We return frequently throughout the book to this common theme of understanding others by looking through their lenses.

Every individual in any organization has the ability to influence others and has a certain amount of power in the organization. The amount of power a person has is a total of the formal power that is given by the position the individual has in the organization plus the amount of informal power individualist has earned. Informal power is based on one's knowledge, expertise, reputation, networks, and interpersonal skills. Formal power is given to an individual by virtue of their position in the organization. By exercising formal power an individual has the ability to reward, punish, and to "tell people what to do." We saw a sign recently in the lobby of a small business. It read, "The boss is always the boss." That sign clearly states the "power" of the boss.

In working with hundreds of project leaders in our seminars, we have come to the simple conclusion that most project leaders do not have the luxury of resorting to formal authority. In most cases, the boss is always the boss, but the project leader is not actually the boss of the project team members. From an academic standpoint, we refer to this situation as a matrix organization in which project leaders cut across functional areas to borrow individual contributors. In some cases, these project leaders at least have the power of allocating budget. But we have also found many organizations in which project leaders do not even allocate budget. They are simply responsible for delivering results while functional managers allocate people and budget.

The bottom line is that most project leaders cut across functional areas to borrow contributors who also have functional responsibilities and report dotted line to other project leaders as well. These project leaders have no choice but to rely on influencing without formal authority since they essentially have none. The closest thing these project leaders have to formal authority is the ability to tap into the formal authority of project sponsors, steering committees, or other decision-making bodies. We have found that even project leaders who are lucky enough to have dedicated project teams get better results from tapping into informal sources of authority than relying on formal authority.

We have been influenced by Allen Bradford and David Cohen who have written an excellent book on the topic of influencing without formal authority.[1] They emphasize the importance of understanding the world of those whom we are trying to influence and present influencing as a process of identifying favorable exchanges. We highly recommend their book to anyone pursuing additional information on how to develop thoughtful influencing strategies.

Seeking Alignment Through Influence

When leading a global project team, one of the first priorities is to seek alignment among team members. Sometimes we hear this referred to as "being on the same page" but whatever we call it, we would like each of our project team members to be helpful and to have a positive impact on our project. We know from practice that such alignment of positive intentions and abilities to impact the project are not always a natural starting point for projects. Consider the following scenario that we use in many of our seminars.

Hans, the project manager for a major quality improvement project aimed at encouraging more sharing of best practices across marketing,

---

[1] Allan R. Cohen and David L. Bradford (2005), "Influence Without Authority," John Wiley & Sons, Inc. Hoboken, New Jersey.

manufacturing, and finance, just met for the first time with his core project team consisting of Brigitte from marketing, Thomas from a consulting organization, James from manufacturing, and Judith from finance. Team members were assigned by influential project sponsors within each business area. Hans, originally from Frankfurt, has been with finance for 3 years.

Brigitte just graduated from Harvard with an MBA. She has 3 years of work experience with McKinsey prior to joining the company last month. She is eager to do a good job. She has also become an instant best friend with Judith and has been working hard to convince Judith that Judith's career has not reached a dead end. Hans has been very impressed with Brigitte's attitude and willingness to support the team. Hans is also keenly aware that Brigitte has very high level mentors at headquarters in Geneva. Before Harvard, Brigitte was a New York native with parents from Denmark.

Judith has become quite negative due to excessive multitasking across multitudes of projects for the past 10 years. She is essentially burnt out and doesn't really want to deal with Hans, the project leader. Judith does not understand why she was assigned to this project steering committee. She would really prefer to focus on her functional responsibilities and tends to place project work at a very low priority in her PalmPilot. Judith was born in Basel.

James, from New Jersey, has significant experience working on prior best practices projects that did not succeed, and he is quite skeptical about this new initiative. He has been with the company for 5 years. James has had several outbursts with Judith and prefers to keep distance from her.

Thomas, the consultant from Geneva, has extensive experience working with other companies on best practice sharing, but he is not convinced that the ambitious goals of the project charter can be achieved and would like to see the project canceled in favor of other projects in the queue. Thomas has worked with Judith on several other successful projects and they have professional respect for one another.

We are often surprised by how many project leaders tell us that their project teams mirror this scenario in many ways. The world is full of dysfunctional teams. You could use this scenario to generate a discussion with your own project team about how to influence key stakeholders. The approach we take in our seminars is to

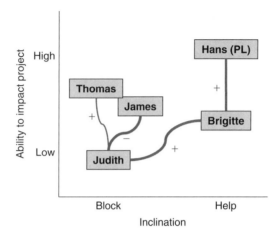

Figure 5.1   Mapping Inclination, Impact, and Relationships.

ask small groups to discuss the scenario for about half an hour and return with thoughts about how to achieve alignment within this project team. The starting point for the exercise, after reading this scenario, is to decide where each team member falls along the continuums of both intention and impact. We can also map relationships using lines and plus or minus signs. Figure 5.1 illustrates the mapping of intentions, impact, and relationships for these project team members.

Influencing Imperative 1

Map stakeholder intentions, power, and relationships.

Given the limited information supplied in this scenario, the exact locations and strength of the relationships as indicated by the thickness of the lines could be debated. Incomplete information aside, this map represents a good starting point for thinking about how Hans would achieve alignment. After all, as project leaders we do not receive a briefing on the intentions and potential impact of each key stakeholder. We need to do some investigating on our own.

Ideally, Hans would like to see each project team member in the upper right-hand quadrant. The upper left-hand quadrant is the most dangerous since the stakeholders in this quadrant are inclined to block the project and they have some power to do so.

If Hans were your friend, what advice would you give him?

_____

_____

_____

_____

_____

_____

When we present this question in an exercise and allow groups of project leaders to debate and then present a solution, we often hear the following advice:

- Fire Thomas. He's a consultant. It's his job to support this project.
- Give Judith a pep talk and pair her with Brigitte, perhaps serving as Brigitte's mentor.
- Find out why James has an issue with Judith.
- Tell James he needs to get on board.
- Give Brigitte lots of work and encourage her to keep giving pep talks to Judith.

After some heated debate, we encourage people to think more deeply about the worlds of Thomas, Judith, Brigitte, and James. What does each of these individuals really want? What cues might we find from the information in this scenario?

The fundamental question is "What's in it for me (WIIFM)?" However, we need to ask this question from the perspective of those whom we are trying to influence. If we are completely honest with ourselves and question why somebody would want to work on our project, we will be well along the path of developing an influencing strategy that will deliver desired results. We want people to work on our projects.

Influencing Imperative 2

Consider "What's in it for me?" from the stakeholders' perspectives. Why would they want to contribute to your project?

In addition to thinking through what individual contributors want, we also need to think about the capabilities these individuals offer to our project. After all, it doesn't make sense to spend a lot of time trying to influence someone if they do not have the capabilities that we need, particularly if we do not have the time or resources to increase their capabilities through training and other development activities.

When we revisit this scenario and think more deeply about each team member's capabilities and WIIFMs, we typically arrive at something that looks like Table 5.1.

Clearly, the project leader, Hans, also wants project success. The questions that he needs to ask include:

1. *What do I need?* The answer to this question is a clear understanding of the project scope, and more specifically from the

Table 5.1 Aligning Capabilities and WIIFM

Team Member	Capabilities	WIIFM?
James	Experience/lessons learned	To be involved in a successful best practices project
Judith	Deep experience	To stop multitasking across so many projects
Brigitte	Analytical business skills and superior presentation abilities	Exposure and promotion
Thomas	Deep experience of what has worked in other companies	Sustainable consulting business

breakdown structure (as described in Chapter 2). It does not make sense to influence anyone until we are very clear about what we need. Influencing is about getting people to act and behave in manners that support achieving our project deliverables.

2. *Can each project team member's capabilities be harnessed to contribute to the project?* Once we are clear on what needs to be done to achieve our project deliverables, we need to scan the capabilities of our actual or potential project team members. If the team members do not have the required skills and knowledge, then we have to consider replacing them or helping them get the capabilities they need.

3. *Can I offer something that the team members need or want?* In most organizations, project leaders cannot offer promotions or significant monetary incentives. But when we dig deeply, we usually find that project team members are often looking to satisfy needs other than those related to short-term monetary gains. In short, they are typically looking for other factors such as recognition, career advancement, security, the ability to acquire new knowledge and skills, social connection, and a host of other potential desires.

Based on the elaboration of wants and needs, our seminar participants have come up with solutions similar to these:

- Pair James and Thomas to review the overall project scope and provide risk management recommendations that might include slicing the overall project scope into much smaller and achievable subprojects. If they question the ability to achieve the objectives, they are perfectly suited to help with risk management. As mentioned in the Shackleton example in Chapter 1, we are well advised to keep these challenging stakeholders close to us.

- Talk with Judith's boss and the project sponsor to have her assigned full-time to the current project. She needs focus, and Hans and the project will benefit from her expertise. Additionally, the problems that James was having with her might have been due to her negative attitude from excessive multitasking.

- Let Brigitte do much of the analytical work and present project status to the steering committee. This utilizes her talents and gives her the exposure that she likely wants.

The straightforward exercise highlights the importance of mapping the stakeholder terrain and looking beyond the surface to consider what would constitute a favorable exchange. After all, anyone we want to influence is, on some level, thinking "WIIFM?"

Influencing Imperative 3

Allow our influencing strategy to be guided by both what I need as a project leader and what key contributors want and need as active participants.

Mapping the stakeholder terrain provides information about stakeholders' intentions and their abilities to impact our projects. This exercise provides information used to target influencing strategies for individuals and stakeholder groups. The critical step involves identifying stakeholders' capabilities and looking through their lenses to understand what it might take to make them feel positively compelled to contribute to the project.

In practice, we find that an influencing strategy must include additional elements including achieving absolute clarity on how the project supports organizational strategy, and understanding in detail what needs to be done. In addition to clarifying the purpose and work of the project before we begin our mapping of the stakeholder terrain and aligning our needs with contributors' capabilities, we may need to target our influencing to key decision-makers. Influencing upward requires getting into the heads of decision-makers and tailoring our approach to specific decision-making styles or profiles.

Developing an Influencing Strategy

We apply a very straightforward model for developing an influencing strategy.

1. *Understand the strategy that the project supports.* As we stated in the introduction of this book, effective global project leaders create project value and strategic alignment. Project results only matter when they support a viable organizational strategy. We need to understand the true value that our project delivers and be willing to subordinate thoughts about scope, schedule, and budget to bigger picture of strategy. It is the strategy that matters. Projects are simply strategy in motion. Without strategic alignment, projects are rudderless.

2. *Identify and clearly communicate what needs to be done.* Again, we cannot develop a sound influencing approach without first understanding what needs to be done. Influencing is about getting others to act and behave in ways that support our project. In addition to simply identifying the work breakdown structure, or scope, of our project we also need to communicate our understanding of what needs to be done to project team members.

3. *Identify and clearly communicate why we are working on the project.* We have yet to identify any individuals who are inspired by work breakdown structures. Well-known leaders such as Mahatma Gandhi, John F. Kennedy, and Martin Luther King moved nations and arguably the world by creating compelling visions. Allowing the team to craft a project vision, using the process that we outlined in Chapter 3, can be a powerful starting point for identifying an inspiring purpose for working on the project.

4. *Map the stakeholder terrain.* The process that we outlined earlier in this chapter for mapping stakeholders' intentions (blocker or supporter) and abilities to impact the project provides a high level overview of the stakeholder terrain. By stakeholder terrain, we mean the big picture that tells us who is with us and against us as well as who really has the power to help or hurt. High powered blockers require the most attention in developing an influencing strategy.

5. *Don't give up before you get started.* In practice, we find that many if not most project leaders deal with difficult blockers by trying to neutralize their influence by ignoring or isolating them. This can be a big mistake. Problems do not disappear when ignored. Isolating blockers can lead to alienation that feeds the blocker's reasons to attack your project.

Recall the story of Shackleton, the great Antarctic explorer who brought his 27 crew members safely back to their countries after spending almost 2 years on the ice. One could imagine during that time there were many negative people, troublemakers, naysayers, or disruptive individuals. Shackleton in virtually all cases brought the troublemakers close to him and considered them as potential supporters or allies. There are always reasons to cooperate with individuals and assuming that a person will be an adversary prevents project leaders from understanding and leads to stereotyping and miscommunication. If one treats an individual as a potential "enemy" the self-fulfilling prophecy frequently results. If one considers an individual as a potential supporter, that individual frequently becomes a supporter. In other words the self-fulfilling prophecy is real in project leadership behaviors.

We have found numerous examples in which project leaders have relied heavily on the knowledge of individual contributors or the support of functional area managers who did not appear to be project supporters. Keep the blockers close.

6. *Look through the lens of the individual whom you are trying to influence.* The information that we provided in Chapter 4 on communicating across cultures will be especially useful here. There is a saying in a small restaurant run by American Indians in the Grand Canyon that says: "Do not judge another person until you have walked one mile in his moccasins." Understanding the world of the people on our team is fundamental for any leader of global projects.

The following poignant example illustrates the need to understand the world of others. A financial analyst, Deborah, was consistently late in providing critical information required to perform certain earned value analyses for a project. Her work involved gathering project cost and schedule information from contractors and functional teams located throughout Europe and Asia. Deborah's work had been accurate and punctual. However, one summer she began making mistakes and missing deadlines. She appeared to be unwilling to provide any reasons for the unusual mistakes and delays. When confronted, she simply apologized and indicated that she would try harder in the future. Several project managers who relied on her reports began complaining to her functional manager. The project managers began finding ways to work around Deborah.

After many weeks of frustration, a senior project manager called a meeting with Deborah and her functional boss. During this meeting, Deborah broke down and began weeping uncontrollably. She said that her husband was terminally ill, and that expenses were not covered by insurance and the pain of slowly losing a husband and father was devastating the family.

The project leaders who had "written her off" led a campaign to cover the medical expenses for the family. This included some challenging of company policies as well as extra efforts such as donating time to run weekend carwashes to raise additional money for the family to cover expenses. Deborah was given time to spend with her husband and family and subsequently returned to deliver her analyses with the accuracy and timeliness that matched her reputation before her world took an unfortunate turn.

Spend the time to diagnose the world of others. This diagnosis could be from a cross-cultural perspective, looking through another's lens, or simply from the perspective of finding out if there are any big changes in the professional and personal lives of project contributors. We're not suggesting that you get overly personal, just that you show enough compassion as a project leader to understand that there's more to the lives of others than contributing to your project. That little bit of understanding goes a long way toward finding favorable exchanges, and even in some cases determining who should be on the project team.

Influencing Imperative 4

Follow the Platinum Rule: Do unto others according to their preferences.

7. *When influencing a decision-maker, tailor your approach to his or her decision-making style.* Influencing project team members to behave in certain ways to support your project differs from influencing decision-makers to take a decision supporting your project. Although one could argue that the notion of deciding "WIIFM?" from the decision-maker's standpoint is still valid, how we present our case to the decision-maker will vary according to the individual's decision-making style.

Our simple questionnaire-based approach for understanding executives' decision-making styles has been adapted from the work of Gary Williams and Robert Miller.[2] These consultants and authors determined that executives have default decision-making styles developed early in their careers. Understanding these default decision-making styles provides an opportunity for tailoring verbal and written messages for maximum impact. Our questionnaire includes cross-cultural dimensions such as the extent to which decisions should be consensus-based as well as considerations such as sensitivity to time and hierarchy.

In order to adapt our presentation style to that of an executive whom we are trying to influence, we need to understand the executive's decision-making style and our own. The short questionnaire in Figure 5.2 provides a set of characteristics that we have found to be very useful in tailoring our message to executives. When working with project leaders, we ask them to circle their level of agreement (AA = strong agreement and DD = strong disagreement) with each of the characteristics as they apply to the decision-maker and underline each of the characteristics as they apply to themselves.

[2] William, G.A. and Miller, A.B. (2002), Change the way you persuade, Harvard Business Review, 80(5), 65–73.

Characteristic	Extent of agreement (circle one)
Wants to examine many different perspectives before making a decision	DD D D/A A AA
Requires extensive data to support any decision	DD D D/A A AA
Relies on a small circle of trusted advisors	DD D D/A A AA
Avoids taking risks	DD D D/A A AA
Tends to rely on approaches that have worked in the past	DD D D/A A AA
Likes to hear illustrative stories	DD D D/A A AA
Prefers action over words	DD D D/A A AA
Usually has his or her mind made up before any project presentation	DD D D/A A AA
Has a good sense of humor	DD D D/A A AA
Loves to talk	DD D D/A A AA
Requires presentation materials in advance	DD D D/A A AA
Has a reputation for being rough on people	DD D D/A A AA
Enjoys novel solutions	DD D D/A A AA
Relies on consensus as a cultural norm for decision-making	DD D D/A A AA
Decisions must be vetted through the entire hierarchy	DD D D/A A AA
Tends toward impatience and quick decisions	DD D D/A A AA
Prefers to establish a relationship before taking a decision on someone's behalf	DD D D/A A AA

Figure 5.2   Decision-Making Style Questionnaire.

We then ask them to place an X next to each characteristic that is AA or DD for the decision-maker and a checkmark next to each AA or DD characteristic for themselves. This provides a quick snapshot of the decision-making style of the person from whom the project leader is seeking a favorable decision and the project leader's style as well.

Consider an example in which you have underlined AA for "Has a good sense of humor" for yourself and circled DD for the decision-maker on the same characteristic. This is a quick indication that the decision-maker is a no-nonsense individual and that you may have to shift your tendency toward humor to a more serious approach. Similarly, if you have identified that the decision-maker is risk-averse but you strongly disagree with yourself being risk-averse, you will need to temper your risk-taking with a detailed description of the risk mitigation strategy that you have put in place so that you do not appear to be at odds with the decision-maker.

Influencing Imperative 5

Adapt your approach to the decision-making style of those whom you are trying to influence.

The seven-step approach for developing an influencing strategy exceeds the effort most project leaders put into thinking about how to influence others. We believe that the time and effort put into developing this type of influencing approach pays big dividends. Beyond the basics of project management, most of what we do as project leaders involves influencing others to support our projects through their work and through taking decisions on our behalf.

Helping more junior project managers, be they intentional or unintentional ones, should be a priority for any organization that has an enlightened view on project-based work. Virtually all work is project work. As you become more skilled in the process of developing influencing strategies and influencing others through both verbal and written communication, take time to teach the craft to others. It has been said that the best leaders are also good teachers. Given some of the demographic shifts that we are seeing in the workplace, a new imperative has been set in many organizations to get younger project managers up to speed as quickly as possible to replace retiring experienced project leaders. The following exercise that we use in our seminars could be adapted for your own use to help develop project leadership talent in your organization.

Influencing Exercise

In our leading global projects seminars, we have an exercise in which participants respond exceedingly favorably. When the exercise is completed, each individual is able to get feedback from colleagues on their abilities to influence using the model. The exercise is as follows. We introduce the activity by reminding participants that our goal during the time we are spending together is to "Create a comfortable, yet challenging atmosphere when global project leaders will be willing to question, share, learn, and change."

There are several parts in the exercise.

Part 1 – Will take about 10 minutes and is to be completed individually and quietly.

Describe in a few sentences one issue/change that you would like to see in your organization regarding how global project management is operationalized. If you cannot identify issue/change in global project management, describe any issue/change that you would like to see in your organization. Then, assuming you have the ability to "influence" four or five people in your organization, who may be from different functions and perhaps different cultures who might support or not support your issue, how would you present your idea? What influencing approaches would you employ?

Part 2 – This is completed in groups of five people. A leader will be assigned. The role of the leader is to be a time keeper and to ensure the procedures outlined are followed. Each person in the group receives 10 chits.

(A) Each person has about 5 minutes to present the issue in Part 1. Others listen.

(B) After each person has presented, the first presenter receives feedback from every member AND a certain number of chits.

Rule: You cannot give the same number of chits to any two individuals. You can, however, decide not to give chits to more than one person.

Part 3 – When individuals return to the main room, they are asked to complete the Influence Without Authority Learning Form on the basis of the number of chits they received and the verbal feedback they heard from the other participants.

Influence Without Authority Learning Form

1. My influencing strengths are:

2. I need to improve:

3. Actions I will take to increase my influencing without authority skills:

In follow-up conversations with many participants, they can specifically recall feedback they had received and actions they are taking to improve their influencing without authority skills. When we ask participants to share why they gave their chits to the winner, we typically hear comments like the following:

- She spoke with passion.
- She focused on what was in it for me.
- She persuaded with both logic and emotion.
- She presented a strong business case.
- She adapted her approach based on our reactions.

Consider using this exercise with one of your project teams. A role-play exercise in which project team members attempt to influence functional subject matter experts on a subject of great significance to the project provides an outstanding opportunity to practice influencing skills. As an alternative exercise, take turns attempting to influence a mock steering committee. By practicing influencing skills and receiving feedback, real progress can be made in improving project leaders' and project team members' abilities to influence important stakeholders.

Influencing Imperative 6

Practice leads to improved influencing skills.

One of the comments that we hear time and time again from those who have been influenced by others is that the one doing the influencing has the ability to read others and adjust the influencing approach. Developing skills in reading nonverbal signals allows us to better influence others.

Reading Nonverbal Signals

To influence effectively without formal authority, project leaders need to be able to read and accurately interpret nonverbal messages. "They may get your signal but not your message." This statement was heard in a public presentation given by an expert in nonverbal communication. He went on to say, after stressing the importance of taking into account the nonverbals in any message (often nonverbals contribute up to half of the meaning), when attempting to influence without authority, across cultures, there are three possibilities:

1. The nonverbal in both cultures has the same meaning. In this case the same message is transmitted.
2. The nonverbal does not mean anything in their culture. In this case, we have rarely seen problems as no nonverbal message is communicated.
3. The nonverbal signal in one culture means something but in the other culture it means something else. This results in misunderstandings and often communication problems for the team.

Look at Figure 5.3 showing four pictures of a Japanese man who is attempting to communicate something "nonverbally." What is he communicating? Then look at the answers. Nine out of ten Japanese who looked at the pictures agreed he was, in fact, communicating these reactions.

Figure 5.3   Reading Nonverbal Cues.

Figure 5.3   *(Continued)*.

Picture one communicates he is angry, upset and does not state this but is attempting to communicate this nonverbally. Picture two communicates excitement ... interest. Picture three also communicates interest . . . you are on the right path. Picture four communicates that he is thinking about it . . . he is not confused but needs a little more time.

Influencing Imperative 7

Read the nonverbal cues when attempting to influence others. Use these nonverbal cues as gauge of your effectiveness and adjust your approach accordingly.

The ultimate test of our ability to influence others often comes from trying to reach an agreement through negotiation. As project leaders, we find ourselves engaged in both formal and informal negotiations on a regular basis. By combining our influencing skills with an understanding of some negotiation best practices, we can become highly skillful in reaching mutually beneficial agreements with stakeholders.

Negotiating in Global Projects

There are many definitions of negotiation. The Latin word "negotiari" comes from two words "neg" meaning not, and "otuim" meaning ease or leisure. In other words negotiating is hard work. Negotiation always involves two or more parties with both common interests and conflicting interests, who enter a process of interacting together with the goal or outcome of reaching some kind of agreement. Skillful negotiators make good judgments, have a patient nature, and listen well to their counterparts' perspectives. Effective negotiators have the ability to find quick responses to unforeseen surprises. The secret in any negotiation is to be able to illustrate the common advantages to both parties and to connect these advantages so they are balanced.

We assume that readers of this book have foundational knowledge in the area of negotiations. Fundamentals include guidelines such as focusing on interests rather than positions to allow some give-and-take in reaching desired outcomes. Our seven-step model for developing an influencing strategy provides a good starting point for identifying interests since we have included clarifying the strategy supported by the project and the specific work required. This is especially useful when we are negotiating for contracted project work. Just as we recommend a thorough grounding in project management fundamentals before leading global projects, we also recommend a more thorough grounding in negotiation fundamentals before refining approaches for cross-cultural negotiations. Our focus will be on approaches, simple models, and tools that you can use to succeed in cross-cultural negotiations required to support global projects.

Many years ago Copeland Griggs suggested a number of practical rules for any international negotiation. We have included the ones we believe are most applicable to leaders of global projects who need to negotiate an issue.

Rule 1: Determine if the issue is negotiable.
Rule 2: Define what "winning" the negotiation means to you.
Rule 3: Understand the facts.
Rule 4: Develop a strategy and decide how to position your proposal.
Rule 5: Select a skillful team.
Rule 6: Allow sufficient time.
Rule 7: Give face.
Rule 8: Without a relationship there is no long-term deal.

We believe that these rules represent a good starting point for preparing for a negotiation. As previously stated, we also have to consider fundamental negotiation practices such as understanding our best alternative to a negotiated agreement and the like. The eagerness to make a deal can overcome the logic of the deal if we don't stick to a set of rules to guide our negotiating preparation and behavior.

Influencing Imperative 8

Develop a set of negotiating rules and stick to the rules to avoid losing sight of the requirements needed for a mutually beneficial agreement.

To better understand the global context of negotiations, we recommend the following framework. We have found that those who follow it in planning for the global aspects of project negotiations are better prepared to deal with the actual phases of the negotiation process.

A Framework for Global Negotiations

Earlier in this chapter we presented a framework or model for planning an influencing strategy. What follows is a framework or model for negotiating. This framework was created to help business people and leaders of global projects participate effectively in global negotiations. It was originally developed by Weiss and Stripp and developed further in *Dynamics of Successful International Business Negotiations* by Moran and Stripp.

The framework distinguishes four components representing key aspects of the negotiation process and is presented in Figure 5.4

Policy defines the interests, the project leader, and the scope of the project.

Interaction is the period of information exchange during which the negotiators propose, offers, and counteroffers.

Deliberation is the process by which the negotiators evaluate the interaction, adjust their understanding of the counterpart's

Framework for Global Business Negotiations

Variables	Negotiator's profile
1. Basic concept of negotiation	strategic ◄───────► synergistic
2. Selection of negotiators	technical ability ◄───────► social skills
3. Role of individual aspirations	organization ◄───────► self
4. Concern with protocol	formal ◄───────► informal
5. Significance of type of issue	substantive ◄───────► relationship-based
6. Complexity of language	verbal ◄───────► nonverbal
7. Nature of persuasive argument	logic ◄──────dogma──────► emotion
8. Value of time	strict ◄───────► relaxed
9. Bases of trust	law ◄───────► friendship
10. Risk-taking propensity	cautious ◄───────► adventurous
11. Internal decision-making systems	authoritative ◄───────► consensus
12. Form of satisfactory agreement	explicit ◄───────► implicit

Figure 5.4 Global Negotiations Framework.

requirements, and reformulate expectations, preferences, and proposals in an effort to resolve conflict interests.

Outcome refers to the final understanding reached by the parties.

This framework divides the 4 components into 12 variables, outlined in Table 5.2, that can influence the success or failure of the negotiation.

By categorizing information under each of these 12 variables, negotiators can develop a profile of what they bring to the

Table 5.2   Components of a Global Negotiation

1.	Policy	Basic Concept of Negotiation Selection of Negotiators Role of Individual Aspirations Concern for Protocol
2.	Interaction	Significance of Issue Complexity of Language Nature of Persuasive Argument Value of Time
3.	Deliberation	Bases of Trust Risk-Taking Propensity Internal Decision Making Systems
4.	Outcome	Form of Satisfactory Agreement

negotiation and what their counterparts bring. Each variable will be briefly explained.

Basic concept of negotiation: Every negotiator is driven by a variety of different beliefs, concepts, and attitudes regarding the approaches to the negotiation process. There are two basic opposing philosophies of negotiation, strategic and synergistic. Under the strategic negotiation model, resources are seen to be limited, that is, there is a fixed pie. Each side wants to get as much of the pie as it can. In synergistic negotiations resources are seen to be unlimited, that is, there is plenty of pie for everyone. Each side wants to get as much pie as it can get and, by cooperating, everyone can have as much as they want.

Selection of negotiators: Negotiators have emotions, deeply held values, and different backgrounds and viewpoints. It is important to know why your negotiating counterparts are negotiating with you.

Role of aspirations: Like all human beings, negotiators have needs that they want to satisfy. Classical economic theory assumes that, as an individual, the negotiator will act in a manner that best fulfills his/her interests. Determining the interests or what is in it for the other person is critical.

Concern with protocol: The rules of protocol may be formal or informal. Negotiators who insist on formal protocol stress adherence to strict and detailed rules that govern manners and conduct. Negotiators who are informal attach little importance to explicit displays of courtesy and are inattentive to rules that govern manners and conduct. If the counterpart's expectations of courteous behavior are not met, confusion and conflict may result. We recommend the following guidelines for influencers and negotiators. If there is the slightest doubt as to behaving formally or informally, err on the side of "too formal." Otherwise damage could result to the relationship.

Significance of type of issue: Defining the issues is one of the most important parts of negotiation. Remember the previous section on "framing the problem in a common way." Sometimes negotiators spend more time in trying to agree what the issues are than in settling them.

Complexity of language: "Context" is the vocal and nonvocal aspects of communication that surround a word or passage and clarify its meaning. Contextual aspects include eye contact, pupil contraction and dilation, facial expression, odor, color including changes in facial tone, hand gestures, body movements, personal distancing, and use of space. The earlier discussion of low/high context communication is relevant here.

Nature of persuasive argument: Aristotle identified three means of influencing belief and action: *logos* (logical appeal); *pathos* (emotional appeal); *ethos* (the appeal that comes from the listener's respect for the speaker as a person). Effective influencers and negotiators use a blend of logos, pathos, and ethos depending on the style and behavior of one's counterparts.

Value of time: A person's orientation to "time" is both individual (unique) and cultural (shared by others). Cultures have different ways of organizing and using time. Some cultures take a strict view of scheduling and others are more relaxed.

Internal decision-making systems: Decisions are often made on the basis of past experience, and personal biases. Decision-making systems can be broadly dichotomized as either "authoritative" or "consensus." In authoritative decision-making systems, leaders make decisions without much concern for consensus. In consensus decision-making systems, negotiators do not have the authority to make decisions without consulting superiors. The team leader must obtain support from team members and listen to their advice.

Risk-taking propensity: Decisions can be made under conditions of certainty, risk, or uncertainty. Risk implies the chance of injury, damage, or loss. Negotiators can be labeled either "cautious" or "adventurous." Uncertainty avoidance means avoiding ambiguous situations rather than avoiding risk. Uncertainty avoiding cultures have a need for structure and dogma.

Bases of trust: Negotiators face the dilemma of trust. Every negotiator must face the issue of having to infer the counterparts' true intentions, interests, and preferences. When the negotiation is governed by mutual trust, the counterparts' behavior can be taken as a true indication of their underlying dispositions. In many ways, negotiators base their trust on either law or friendship.

Form of satisfactory agreement: There are two forms of satisfactory agreement. One is explicit, detailed written contract that, by covering all contingencies, requires no future cooperation and binds the parties through an outside enforcement mechanism. The other is an implicit, broad oral agreement that, in accepting unforeseen change as normal, leaves room for the parties to deal with the problem and binds them through the quality of their personal relationship.

Influencing Imperative 9

Take cultural differences into account when negotiating. Use the global negotiations framework.

This negotiating framework will be helpful to any leader of a global project when influencing without authority or negotiating with team members, steering committees, or any stakeholder. The following checklist, summarized in Table 5.3, can be used as a guide before the negotiation and in the face-to-face interaction.

Table 5.3 Negotiation Checklist

Preparation Checklist
Please consider the following
1. Purpose of the meeting.
2. Departments and individuals involved.
3. Issues to be negotiated.
4. Objectives of the negotiation.
5. Review of background information before the negotiation.
6. Discussion of the roles of people and the strategy to be used.
7. Now discuss the above six points from your negotiating counterpart's perspective.

We strongly believe in the use of tools such as checklists and simple models. Straightforward checklists and simple models such as the summary of 12 variables for negotiations outlined in Figure 5.5, on the following page, provide guidance especially when we are preparing for negotiation and potentially even flying into another time zone to conduct the negotiation. When we developed our basic influencing strategy, we were careful to look at the wants and needs and decision-making styles of those who were influencing through their lenses. Negotiations are structured influencing sessions. By considering 12 variables that impact negotiation from our perspective and 12 variables impacting the negotiation from our counterpart's perspective, we are preparing beyond the negotiations fundamentals such as best alternatives to negotiated agreements (BATNA) and must-haves that could trigger walking away points.

Regardless of our skills in influencing and negotiating, we will face inevitable conflict from time to time. As skillful global project leaders, we seek opportunities to turn conflict into cooperation.

Influencing Without Authority and Turning Conflicts into Cooperation

We begin with some proverbs.

Say what you mean and mean what you say – American
It is good to know the truth, but it is better to speak of palm trees – Arab

SUMMARY OF THE TWELVE VARIABLES
FOR OUR NEGOTIATIONS

1. WHAT NEGOTIATING IS:
   distributive bargaining / joint problem-solving / debate / contingency
   bargaining / nondirective-discussion

2. HOW NEGOTIATORS ARE SELECTED:
   knowledge / negotiating experience / personal attributes / status

3. ISSUES DISCUSSED ARE:
   substantive / relationship-based / procedural / personal-internal

4. PROTOCOL
   Informality ———————————▶ formality

5. CONTEXT (use of language)
   low ◀——————————— high

6. HOW ARGUMENTS ARE SOLVED:
   empirical reason / experience / dogma / emotion / intuition

7. TEAM MEMBERS ARE:
   Individual ———————————▶ group

8. HOW TRUST IS ESTABLISHED:
   external sanctions / past record / intuition

9. RISK TAKING
   high ———————————▶ low

10. TIME USE
    monochronic ———————————▶ polychronic

11. DECISIONS ARE:
    authoritative ———————————▶ consensus

12. AGREEMENT IS:
    contractual ———————————▶ implicit

SUMMARY OF THE TWELVE VARIABLES
FOR THEIR NEGOTIATIONS

1. WHAT NEGOTIATING IS:
   distributive bargaining / joint problem-solving / debate / contingency
   bargaining / nondirective-discussion

2. HOW NEGOTIATORS ARE SELECTED:
   knowledge / negotiating experience / personal attributes / status

3. ISSUES DISCUSSED ARE:
   substantive / relationship-based / procedural / personal-internal

4. PROTOCOL
   informality ———————————▶ formality

5. CONTEXT (use of language)
   low ◀——————————— high

6. HOW ARGUMENTS ARE SOLVED:
   empirical reason / experience / dogma / emotion / intuition

7. TEAM MEMBERS ARE:
   individual ———————————▶ group

8. HOW TRUST IS ESTABLISHED:
   external sanctions / past record / intuition

9. RISK TAKING
   high ———————————▶ low

10. TIME USE
    monochronic ———————————▶ polychronic

11. DECISIONS ARE:
    authoritative ———————————▶ consensus

12. AGREEMENT IS:
    contractual ———————————▶ implicit

Figure 5.5   Variable for Our and Their Negotiation.

Hear one and understand ten – Japanese
Silence produces peace and peace produces safety. – Swalili
The first to raise their voices loses the argument – Chinese

Why is conflict included in a book on leading global projects? Simply because every leader of a global project we have interviewed over the past 20 years has stated that every project has some conflicts. Managing conflict is a major organizational issue at the interpersonal, inter-group, and inter-organizational level. Poorly managed conflicts decrease the likelihood of the success of any project.

What is Conflict?

Conflict occurs in situations when the concerns of two parties appear to be incompatible and begins when one party perceives that the other party has frustrated, or is about to frustrate a concern. Cross-cultural conflict occurs in conditions where the concerns of two parties from different cultures appear to be incompatible to one or both of the cultures.

Historically in the West, conflict management within organizations has been viewed in a number of ways. First, conflict was seen as BAD, and to be avoided if at all possible. Now conflict is seen as having functional and beneficial aspects if managed well. Conflict has functional *aspects*. The benefits to the project if conflict is managed well are:

- It clears the air.
- It leads to new ways for handling relationships.
- It can equalize the power between individuals.

Kilman and Thomas have done a significant amount of research on conflict and have developed a widely used conflict mode instrument. Their instrument identifies five ways to deal with conflicts as seen in Figure 5.6.

The *competing* style is the most traditionally Western mode and emphasizes personal achievement. Competing is assertive and

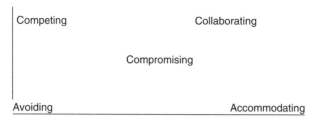

Figure 5.6   Ways to Deal with Conflicts on Projects.

power-oriented mode whereby one uses whatever power seems appropriate to win one's own position.

Accommodating is a more traditionally Asian mode of handling conflict. When accommodating, an individual neglects his/her own concerns to satisfy the concerns of the other person and yields to another's point of view.

Avoiding is also a more traditionally Eastern than Western mode of conflict management. In avoiding conflict an individual does not address the conflict. Avoiding might take the form of diplomatically sidestepping an issue or postponing the discussion of an issue.

Compromising is a mode that attempts to reflect both individual goals. The objective of compromising is to find some expedient, mutually acceptable solution that partially satisfies both parties.

When one *collaborates*, one attempts to recognize both parties' goals while finding solutions that fully satisfy both. It means digging into an issue to identify the underlying concerns of the two individuals and to find an alternative that meets both sets of concerns. It means digging deep into "WIIFM and the other person."

There is no single best style for managing conflict. The important thing to realize is that there are some cultural predispositions such as the Western tendency of competing versus the Eastern tendency of avoiding. We have found that failing to approach and conduct the negotiation through the cultural lens of the person on the other side of the table causes as many or more problems in negotiations as failing to follow negotiation fundamentals. In fact, we would argue that understanding conflict modes from a cross-cultural standpoint should be part of any set of negotiation fundamentals. Dealing effectively with cross-cultural conflict depends on planning for differences and then negotiating with these differences in mind.

Influencing Imperative 10

Understand the conflict mode of those with whom you are negotiating or attempting to influence. This understanding will guide the process of mediating conflict and achieving desired results.

Conclusion

We have presented several models that can be used to map the stakeholder terrain, plan an influencing strategy, plan a cross-cultural negotiation, and recognize different conflict modes when mediating inevitable conflict. We've also presented some exercises and references for application and digging deeper.

The following ten "Influencing Imperatives" provide a quick reference to the key ideas and approaches presented in this chapter. We encourage you to keep these imperatives in an accessible location and to take the time to view the world through the lens of those whom we are influencing or with whom we are negotiating. This repeated cultural theme of understanding the world through the lens of another is perhaps the most important underpinning of effective global project leadership.

Influencing Imperatives

1. Map stakeholder intentions, power and relationships.

2. Consider "What's in it for me?" from the stakeholders' perspectives. Why would they want to contribute to your project?

3. Allow our influencing strategy to be guided by both what I need as a project leader and what key contributors want and need as active participants.

4. Follow the Platinum Rule: Do unto others according to their preferences.

5. Adapt your approach to the decision-making style of those whom you are trying to influence.

6. Practice leads to improved influencing skills.

7. Read the nonverbal cues when attempting to influence others. Use these nonverbal cues as gauge of your effectiveness and adjust your approach accordingly.

8. Develop a set of negotiating rules and stick to the rules to avoid losing sight of the requirements needed for a mutually beneficial agreement.

9. Take cultural differences into account when negotiating. Use the global negotiations framework.

10. Understand the conflict mode of those with whom you are negotiating or attempting to influence. This understanding will guide the process of mediating conflict and achieving desired results.

6

What Project Team Members Need from Us

I have been successful at leading global projects but managing my portfolio is
difficult and I don't spend enough time with my individual teams.
A leader of global projects

Leading projects have been great experiences for me.
A leader of global projects

We begin this chapter with a story of Joe Brown and Paulo Bock who worked together on a global team for a number of years. They also worked together on specific "projects." However, Paulo resigned from the company. This case is used in many of our workshops with leaders of global projects and generates good discussions. Following the case is a list of questions.

This is a situation where a relationship failed and the organization lost a talented individual. But, did they? Were there some flaws in Paulo's character or training? We have observed similar examples on many global teams not only when a member resigns from the company, which is rare for many reasons, but when an individual on the team does not perform at a high level.

The Case of the Brazilian Caddie[1]

"Very well, Tom. I guess we have our man. It really took me some time to teach him how to find his way around New Brunswick, but he is intelligent and with a little more mentoring and coaching, I think we have found our man.

Joe Brown finished his telephone conversation with the Latin America Human Resources director and started to think about his next conversation with Paulo Bock, his best sales manager and successor to the Vice Presidency of Sales.

Joe thought he had already paid his dues. Four years in a subsidiary was a long time, and more than the usual assignment of other

---

[1]This case was written by Marcos Dutra, MIM, under the supervision of Robert T. Moran, PhD. It is based on several business relationships which failed.

expatriates from Julius Foods. Most of his peers would only spend 2 years abroad, and Joe was very concerned about the effects of staying away from headquarters for so long. Not that Joe didn't have a good relationship with the people in New Jersey; he called them frequently and made sure that he would visit at least once every 2 months. Joe was very conscious of the need to show his face and touch base with the right people, so he would have a nice position when he needed to return to the United States following his success in Brazil.

Brazil had been an exciting and challenging experience for Joe. The country was developing quickly and the competition was brutal. All the multinational companies he knew from the States were here, and also some others from Europe, not to mention the local ones. They were taking whatever they could from this big, but not infinite market. It took Joe at least 1 year to understand all the complexity of the country, and he was still amazed of how many differences there were in the consumption habits of the several regions. It made him envy the easy job some of his friends had managing the Sales department of the company in smaller countries.

Joe knew that one of his most important tasks would be to develop a successor. The company was convinced for some time that in a globalized world, talent should be groomed and nurtured wherever it could be found. Expatriates were necessary to establish the company's corporate culture in the country, but they were surely expensive. That was one of the reasons corporate HR was so resolute in this objective of achieving a majority of Brazilians in the directors' board. They were expecting that the new reality would motivate promising local professionals to work hard, since there would be no glass ceiling" preventing their promotions.

Paulo Bock was an essential element in this plan. His results had been very good, and his talent had caught the attention of the right people, especially after his time in New Jersey. He had started his career working for one of the largest distributors in Brazil, where he knew firsthand how the difficult sales market worked. Later he joined the staff of a competitor in the Marketing department and moved back to Sales when he came to Julius Foods, 4 years ago. Joe quickly realized his talent, and was one of the biggest motivators in his decision to pursue an MBA in the United States. He realized that this international experience would be fundamental for Paulo's development and for his chances within the company. Joe knew very well how hard it was for someone without these skills to move up, but he was not able to sponsor Paulo's studies. He only assured Paulo of a job when he came back.

Paulo completed his degree in 1 year and after a short time in New Jersey, started working as the national sales manager for the most important division of the company. Combining his new skills with his knowledge of the market, Paulo achieved goals that Joe was only expecting to see 2 years in the future. New Jersey had started tracking him since his internship, and now it was obvious for them that he was the ideal candidate to take Joe's place as Vice President when he came back.

However, Joe was not entirely convinced. Paulo had expressed several times his disbelief in some of the guidelines from the company and made some comments in a recent workshop that were really not appropriate for a senior executive. It was not everyday that a consultant from New Jersey would come to give a presentation to the local team, especially one on an important point like the new sales system the US division had implemented last year. Paulo questioned several points and practically made it clear that such a system would not work in Brazil unless the subsidiary made a lot of changes in it. No matter how right Paulo were, this kind of attitude could be a serious problem for his reputation in New Jersey. Joe had learned the hard way to play the game and he had a feeling that Paulo had still much to learn. His willingness is siding with the sales team against some of the company's directives had been another problem. Paulo was convinced that the team's motivation was the reason of the sales increase, and that a Sales department in Brazil should be run with total openness and informality, even if this philosophy was different from the one the company used in the United States.

Joe had much to lose if Paulo didn't adapt to the new position. After all, Paulo was his responsibility. And now he was really concerned about his decision, especially after hearing from Jim Elliot, the US Logistics Director Paulo escorted to a visit to a big client. Jim missed an important meeting, and blamed Paulo for it.

Wondering how he would address the subject, Joe called Paulo on the phone and suggested a meeting for the end of the day. "Better this way, so he will know it is important," Joe thought. "I hope I can make my point, because he will be the man sitting on my chair."

Later, Paulo entered his office with a smile. "Make yourself comfortable," Joe said in his broken Portuguese. "You must be wondering why I called you this evening. You know we have talked a lot about the challenges you will find in this position when I am gone, but I would not be comfortable if I didn't talk to you one more time. And this time, I will open my heart as a friend, because I really want you to be very successful."

Paulo smiled, not really feeling comfortable with the compliment. Joe went on: "I've been very satisfied with your work and I can't deny that you are the best manager I have under my supervision. I'm especially satisfied with the way you were able to apply the skills you learned at your MBA in your work and the way you deployed this knowledge with your subordinates. To tell you the truth, I was a little skeptical about the results you would get from the training program you implemented with your team, but you certainly proved me wrong. You have the stuff sales managers are made from, the connection with the sales team, and the ability to identify with the client." Joe continued: "However, when you move up to this position, you will be entering a different world. You won't have the time you do now to talk to the team and you will only be able to visit your main clients. Your first priority will be your relationship with the board and the people in New Jersey. You see, you will have to travel at least once every 2 months."

"I hope you will have some time for me when I go to the United States." Paulo joked.

"I certainly will, Paulo. But let me finish this … the other important responsibility you will have will be to escort people from New Jersey when they visit, and this brings me to the point I wanted to bring to your attention." Paulo frowned, trying to guess what the bad news would be. "Jim Elliot and I had a conversation last Monday, and he is still upset because he missed his meeting with the Regional President. I know you can't be blamed for the storm that hit that day, but this kind of situation cannot happen again when you are the new Vice President."

Paulo defended himself – "Joe, you know this client is one of the most important for us. He invited Jim to his farm and this was something we could not deny. The client would be very upset if he didn't go…he even arranged for a helicopter to pick up Ken so he wouldn't miss his plane. Joe, this man built the largest wholesaling company in Latin America in only 30 years, starting with a small rented truck. He is proud of his humble origins and still has a very traditional way of doing business. Being invited to his farm meant that he trusted us. And you know very well that his company is buying more from us than they ever did before."

"Anyway, Jim felt he had no option but to go, and you don't put a director like him in such a position" Joe replied, a little upset.

"As you said, we could not predict the storm. There was no way for the helicopter to come and the car trip really took longer than we thought." Paulo explained. "But I still think that the visit was worthwhile."

"Paulo, I don't think you are getting my point" … Joe said, now changing to English. "Situations like that one can't keep on happening. People take notes about what they see, and this can be detrimental to your future in the organization. I understand that results are the reason we exist for, but there is a corporate culture that can't be denied. After all, this is an American company, and people will judge you with American standards, and one of them is the respect to rules. They appreciate the Brazilian way to create alternatives, the famous 'jeitinho' that always finds a solution for problems, but you will have to understand that this phase of your career is gone. You have outgrown this phase. It is nice to have success, but success means you will have to give up some things you cherish. For example, I can't see a Vice President playing soccer with the employees: it is about time you learn to play golf."

With these words, Joe thought he had sent his message. There was nothing more he could do now; he had to trust that Paulo had heard the voice of reason and that he would try his best. He offered Paulo a glass of the scotch bottle he kept for special guests in his office, but Paulo declined, excused himself and left.

Next morning, Joe could not miss the way people were staring at him and the uncomfortable "good mornings" he was getting from staff. After entering his room, he called Martha, his secretary, and asked: "What is happening this morning? People are behaving strangely. Is there anything I should know?" Martha replied: "It sounds like you haven't read Paulo's e-mail yet. He probably wrote from his house, since it was already here in the computer this morning." "My e-mail is for you, with a copy to all regional managers and the President. Of course, the word is spreading like wild fire in the office. I guess it is better if you read it yourself."

To: Mr. Joe Brown
From: Paulo Bock
Cc: Regional Managers, Presidency
Ref. Meeting with Sales VP

Mr. Brown,
I hope you don't mind I'm writing this e-mail in Portuguese. After all, this is the language of this country, and I guess that after four years, you should be able to understand a little of it.

I thank you for the incentive you gave me to go to your country and get a higher degree in my education. But there is one point that may have escaped your attention. My first objective in getting an MBA was to acquire knowledge and skills that I could later apply in my country, in order to improve the living conditions of the people by doing my part. You see, I believe in the potential of this country. It is fabulously rich, with creative and intelligent people and it has a varied and wonderful culture, like few countries could claim. Brazilians have original music, and excel in literature and movies. Their cultural wealth is recognized throughout the world. And all this was here well before multinational companies arrived.

However, I admit that business is now a universal language. You disagree with my position of adapting the company's guidelines to best fit the Brazilian market, and I can understand your behavior because of your background. You criticize my relationship with the sales team because you think it is a Latin characteristic of too much intimacy, something bad for business. You accuse me of being centered in the Brazilian way of doing things. But I don't do things in a certain way because I am Latin; it is because I think this is the best way to bring results to the company in this environment.

When I visit a client in the country, in small towns, I appreciate his traditions and his habits. This could mean a visit to his farm. If I visit a client that runs a virtual supermarket in the Internet, I choose another approach, maybe a discussion about this week's Nasdaq performance. But both approaches are Brazilian.

I believe my heritage is valuable and could be used with good results by any company, but I think it is sad if Brazilians must cease to be Brazilians to be someone in Julius Foods: this is basically what you are asking from me. This is something I can't do for you, and I'm sure that any citizen of this country with one gram of pride left in his heart will agree with me. That's why I must finish my relationship with this company.

I wish you a nice trip and I hope you enjoy your golf games. Excuse, but today I have a soccer game to attend.

Sincerely,

Paulo Bock

Having read the case, consider the following questions.

1. What is your assessment of Joe Brown as team leader? His strengths? His liabilities?
2. Can Joe Brown overcome his liabilities? If yes, how?
3. What is your opinion of Paulo Bock's reaction? Was it predictable?
4. Would you recommend trying to get Bock to reconsider his resignation? Why or why not?
5. What do you do when you observe the behaviors of a person like Joe Brown or Paulo Bock on a team you are leading or are a member of?

Global Project Teams: A Primer

"High performance teams," "team work," "global project teams," and other words expressing similar ideas are commonplace in the management literature today. Stories of teams producing remarkable accomplishments are well known. Well-functioning teams can be very instrumental in the success of any global project.

The dictionary defines a team as a number of persons working in some joint action. The more team members have in common, the easier it is to develop a team culture. However, when one crosses cultures and tries to assimilate outsiders into a team, development becomes more complicated – even when all the team members are part of the same global organization.

Cultural diversity within a project team increases potential quality of the team's work. Anytime we can work successfully at the intersection of different ways of thinking, we will get better ideas. But the process has to be managed carefully. Cultural diversity, be it functional or country, increases the complexity of communication and decision-making processes. Thus, culturally diverse teams have potential for higher productivity than culturally homogeneous groups, but greater risk of loss arising from a faulty process.

Imperative 1

Whenever you can, make your teams as diverse as possible – diversity in male/female, in national cultures, in functions and in technical skills. Celebrate the ideas and results that come from this diversity.

When we are considering the various challenges and opportunities in managing culturally diverse global project teams, we need to continue to follow the advice threaded through this book – to take the extra time to look through the lens of another rather than assume that our way is the right way and the only way to get things done. When we put our team together, we need to consider the various stages of team development.

Stages of Team Development

A team is an interdependent group of individuals who generally agree on a goal and the way they will accomplish their objective. Most agree that teams go through stages.

1. *Forming*: Group members are often unclear on the exact purpose of the team or the scope of the project and become more familiar with new teammates.
2. *Storming*: Characterized by conflict, in this stage members express frustrations and learn to deal with differences to accomplish their goals.
3. *Norming*: In this stage, project team members become more comfortable working with each other and with the group's methods for completing the tasks.
4. *Performing*: Team members are now ready to get down to the task at hand. They understand the rules and roles of the team and begin to emphasize achieving results.

This well accepted framework for thinking about how teams evolve over time appears to be ignored in many organizations. As global project leaders, we need to be able to recognize these stages and help our team members work their way through each of them. These stages are indeed fundamental and surely familiar, but it is worth spending a moment to think about how we would exercise our leadership to help team members get to the performing stage without necessarily sidetracking some of the important benefits of the earlier stages.

In the *forming* stage, it's our job to help project team members make sense of their participation in the project. Recall our chapter on telling the project story. When we pull the project team together, we need to spend the extra time clarifying the project scope (what we plan to deliver and how we will get the work done), the project value (how the project contributes to the overall objectives of the organization), and the project vision. As the project leader, it's your job to communicate the project value. You will certainly need help to identify the details of how the project deliverables will be achieved, and it's a good idea to make the visioning session as participative as possible.

The *storming* stage is where most mistakes are made. During this stage, project leaders have an opportunity to use unavoidable conflict as a risk management tool. Conflict helps us identify risks, or potential future problems. Use the information embedded in project team members' arguments about the project purpose and approaches to develop risk mitigation strategies and contingency plans. We can even use the information to completely alter our work breakdown structure to follow an entirely different approach to achieve our project deliverables.

Less experienced project leaders often make the mistake of intervening and imposing their will to avoid prolonged debate. Consider the case of Roberto, a project team member on a project that would consolidate multiple divisions' finance operations into a shared services organization in Budapest. Roberto, an Assistant Controller for one of the divisions, argued during one of the initial project meetings that significant changes would have to be made to the accounting practices within each division before, not after, the finance operations were transferred to the shared services organization. Roberto argued that division-level and country-level differences in basic gathering, processing, and reporting of financial data needed to be addressed before attempting to consolidate operations under a single roof in Budapest.

The project leader acknowledged Roberto's concern, but he made it clear during the meeting that the timeline had been established and that they were under strict marching orders to make this happen. Some of the harmonization of the processes would have to be done after the work was transferred to the shared services organization.

The end of the story is predictable. The shared services organization nearly crippled the multinational organization's ability to perform basic financial reporting and put the organization at risk with respect to Sarbanes-Oxley compliance. Spending a small additional amount of time to hear the full debate could have led to some minor rescoping of the effort to mitigate risks that did indeed occur and resulted in significant pain and costs for this organization.

The *norming* stage represents a process of settling in and getting comfortable with each other's approaches. Project leaders can facilitate norming, after working through the storming stage, by providing multiple opportunities for close contact. If the team is dedicated to the project rather than matrixed in from other functional organizations, consider an open space work environment. We found that the best way to understand how other team members work is to be in very close contact. If physical proximity is not possible, picking up the telephone is the next best approach. We recommend videoconferencing only if you have technology that can allow spontaneous connections. Scheduling weekly videoconference meetings tends to be more of a drag on the organization than a benefit.

In a large global pharmaceutical organization, two individuals found themselves assigned as co-project leaders for a major IT project aimed at globalizing certain aspects of HR. One of the co-leaders was from the IT organization and the other was from HR. They chose an open workspace environment for their team and highlighted the significance of this decision by sitting across from each other, literally face-to-face. They found that this process of having constant interaction allowed them to fully understand each other's point of view and learn each other's working styles. Ultimately, they learned to trust each other's abilities and count on each other to fulfill agreed-upon obligations using their own approaches and subject matter expertise. The process of being close to one another accelerated the norming stage and pushed the entire team quickly into the performing stage.

The *performing* stage is the autobahn of projects. As project leaders, our job is to remove any barriers that could get in the way of project team members' abilities to get their work done. One of the biggest barriers that we have identified in the performing stage is the inability of project team members to focus their attention on the task at hand. There are simply too many distractions in most organizations. Most project team members report solid line to functional boss and dotted line to several project leaders. In some cases, what project team members really need from us as project leaders is permission to focus their attention on our project for a period of time.

A Day in the Life of a Project Team Member

You know the feeling. You're trying to save time by doing two or three things at once – sending e-mail to a project team leader while on the phone with your functional boss.

Suddenly, your brain crashes. It can't recall what you just did, what was just said. The project manager who just walked into your cubicle is awaiting a response – to what? You can hardly even recognize the young project manager much less remember what you promised her just last week.

Just as you clear your thoughts, the phone rings and a high priority e-mail flashes across your monitor.

Multitasking Makes You Stupid*

There's scientific evidence that multitasking is extremely hard for some to do, and sometimes impossible. Chronic high stress multitasking also is linked to short-term memory loss.

Having two projects to work on can increase efficiency, but adding a third and more projects the efficiency drops.

The process of switching back immediately to a task you've just performed, as many multitaskers try to do, takes longer than switching back after a bit more time has passed. The brain has to overcome "inhibitions" it imposed on itself to stop doing the task in the first place; it takes time, in effect, to take off the brakes.

People who are multitasking too much experience various warning signs; short-term memory problems can be one. Intense multitasking can induce a stress response, an adrenaline rush that when prolonged can damage cells that form new memory.

*Adapted from material found in "Multitasking Makes You Stupid, Studies Say," Sue Shellenbarger, *The Wall Street Journal*, March 1, 2003.

Perhaps the greatest challenge of the 21st century is that of finding ways to keep our team members and ourselves from becoming "stupid" from too much multitasking. Project team members need to focus during the performing stage of a project, but we live in a world in which focus is a luxury. Anything we can do to help team members reduce the bombardment they receive on a regular basis to their ability to focus attention on our project will produce substantial benefits.

A project leader named Olivier, heading a due diligence team that was examining the potential partnership with a smaller research-based company, tried a new approach to completing his due diligence report. The project team consisted of members from many different functions who lived squarely in the world of multitasking. Olivier knew that the biggest challenge to completing the due diligence report was not the actual due diligence process that included research and a site visit. The problem occurred when the team members completed the site visit and then went back to their functional jobs. Getting them to contribute their portion of the overall due diligence report was like pulling teeth. They simply got back to their regular job and disappeared.

Olivier realized that the actual process of writing the report took no more than a couple of days but that this effort tended to spread out over several months. His somewhat radical approach involved sequestering the team in a hotel for 3 days after the due diligence site visit. The team members agreed that they would work only on the due diligence report until it was completed. It worked. Olivier managed to reduce the time to develop the due diligence report from 3 months to 3 days by focusing the attention of the team on nothing but the report.

We may not want to head down the path of holding our team members captive in hotels to get them to focus on our project, but anything we can do to allow them to focus on our project without the distractions that bombard them on a regular basis will allow the team to achieve breakthrough performance.

As we work our way through the different stages of project team dynamics, we need to consider team player styles. "The contributor" is task and results oriented, with a heavy emphasis on information gathering. "The collaborator" is concerned about the team's mission and tends to focus on the big picture. "The communicator" is interested in maintaining good relationships between all team players and wants to make sure that all members are heard and valued. "The challenger" is problem oriented and is not afraid to question the wisdom of the group.

Although we need to leverage each of the roles throughout the stages, certain team member roles are more important during each stage. We depend on collaborators during the forming stage. These individuals can influence others to see the big picture. Challengers help us raise issues during the storming stage. Contributors help drive the performance during the performing stage, and communicators help us throughout the entire project. By identifying project team member's styles, we can allow them to share in the leadership of the project team by leveraging their strengths in the appropriate stages of team development.

Imperative 2

Project team members needs evolve over the life of the project. If we recognize this, we can plan for changing needs and allow for shared leadership.

Effective teams are characterized by people of diverse backgrounds, talents, and personalities. Team members are interdependent, and we need to ensure that they all reach agreement on the scope of the project and the best way to achieve the objectives.

Research on Project Synergy

At the Culture Learning Institute at the East West Center in Honolulu, Hawaii researchers studied project team effectiveness on international projects. In Figure 6.1 the factors that foster or hinder professional synergy within a project team are listed.

- How project business is planned.

- Consideration of other problem-solving viewpoints.

- How the work should be organized.

- Approach to R&D tasks.

- Definition of R&D problems.

- Ambiguity resolution and problem formulation.

- Methods and procedures.

- Decision-making relative to recurring problems.

- Allocation of resources to team members.

- Accountability procedures relative to resource use.

- Timing and sequencing approaches.

- Determining objectives for an R&D effort.

- Affiliation and liaison with external groups and degree of formality in their work relations.

- Quantity and type of project human resources.

- Qualifications, recruitment, and selection of new members.

- New member orientation and training on the project.

- Management of responsibilities.

- Underutilization of workers relative to skill competencies.

- Motivating behavior and reward expectations.

- Coordination of long/ short-term members.

- Agreement on degree of innovation required.

- Experience with cooperation especially relative to international R&D tasks.

- Official language(s) to use on project.

- Method of reporting every one's involvement in the project.

- Coping with internal demands and visitors.

- Meeting face-to-face and having to resort to other forms of more impersonal communication.

- Involvement in making viewpoints known.

- Power differences because of institution resources brought to the project.

- Prestige, risk-taking, tolerance of uncertainty, and perceptions.

- Project leadership and/or organizational policies changing unexpectedly.

- Quality of work presented in evaluation methods.

- What constituted success in project work, and what to do when members fail to meet group expectations.

- Clarification of roles on the relationships.

Figure 6.1   Human Factors that Foster or Hinder Professional Synergy Within a Project.

In the same study researchers identified the following team member behaviors that are conducive to effective team functioning. The behaviors are:

- Flexibility and openness to change and others' viewpoints.
- Exercising patience, perseverance, and professional security.

- Thinking in multidimensional terms and considering different sides of the issues.
- Dealing with ambiguity, role shifts and differences in personal and professional styles or social and political systems.
- Managing stress and tension well, while scheduling tasks systemically.
- Cross-cultural communication and demonstrating sensitivity to language problems among colleagues.
- Anticipating consequences of one's own behavior.
- Dealing with unfamiliar situations and lifestyle changes.
- Dealing well with different organizational structures and policies.
- Gathering useful information related to future projects.

You can use the above list as a starting point for positive team behaviors. Depending on your particular project, other behaviors might be even more important. What really matters is that you have spent the time thinking about what behaviors you want from the project team members. Some of these behaviors are task oriented while others are more aimed toward team cohesiveness and capability building.

Whatever list you might form, find a way to encourage positive team behaviors. Simple recognition of these positive behaviors goes a long way. This recognition can be in front of the group, or, better yet, a quick face-to-face acknowledgment or phone call. Catch someone doing something particularly well and recognize them on the spot.

Imperative 3

Recognize project team members for their positive behaviors. This simple process of recognition produces a lengthy stream of performance dividends.

Leading Global Projects Quiz

Trivial Pursuit™ is a board game that has sold millions of copies throughout the world. The game requires players to answer questions in a number of categories such as geography, entertainment, history, art and literature, science, and nature and sports. The category of the question is determined by a roll of the dice.

We would like to invite you, the reader, to play this game. You have rolled the dice and drawn the category "Leaders of Global Projects." This is your question: "Which countries produce the most competent leaders of global projects?"

Is the answer Japan? Japan indeed has a successful track record of best-selling products, including cars, electronic equipment, and steel, among others. This is largely accomplished through Japanese businessmen who work for the giant Japanese trading companies – the *sogo shosha*.

Is the answer the United States? The United States is the biggest economic entity in the history of the world, with dominant positions worldwide in computers, space, medicine, biology, and so on. But some say that Americans are naïve internationally and American business people may be the most ethnocentric of all.

Is it Sweden? But Sweden is too small and the Swedish economy has declined sharply since the late 1970s because Swedish internationalists aren't aggressive enough.

The question is indeed a tough one. At a recent meeting of global business leaders attending a seminar on international joint ventures, we posed the same question. It evoked considerable discussion but no agreement.

Hari Bedi, an Indian expatriate who worked for a large multinational company in Hong Kong, believes that Asian global project leaders use the 5 Cs of *continuity* (a sense of history and tradition), *commitment* (to the growth of the organization), *connections* (where social skills and social standing count), *compassion* (balancing science and political issues), and *cultural sensitivity* (a respect for other ways).

These qualities are among the contributions made by Asian managers to a multinational organization, he says. Western global project leaders, according to Bedi, use the 5 Es: *expertise* (experience in managerial and technical theory), *ethos* (practical experience), *eagerness* (the enthusiasm of the entrepreneur), *esprit de corps* (a common identity), and *endorsement* (seeks unusual opportunities).

The answer is that project leaders of every country contribute. The usefulness of that contribution depends on the ability of the project leader to eliminate barriers to intrinsic motivation that all team members possess. This requires a level of understanding similar to that required to develop an influencing strategy, as described in Chapter 5. Global project leaders need to ask the "What's in it for me (WIIFM)?" question from the perspective of each project team member.

Imperative 4

Ask and then answer the "What's in it for me?" question from the perspective of each team member from his or her cultural lens.

A Framework for Identifying What Blocks Motivation and Performance

Consider the case of Max Hoffman and Anne Bremicker. What would you do if you were Anne Bremicker? Would you schedule the meeting with a senior project sponsor?

Max's Bad Attitude

As Anne Bremicker, the project leader for the new flexible factory, entered Max Hoffman's office to ask him for status on some of the proposed production processes, she could sense something was wrong with Max. She shared the good news about being ahead of schedule with the new "Launch Plant" that would be able to manufacture three different new drugs, a flexible hedge against pipeline uncertainties. Max did his best job of forcing a smile and said, "Good news, but we've been ahead before and still managed to screw everything up. There's still a lot of work to be done, and were facing a lot of unknowns. And no matter how well we do, those lower life forms in procurement will never get it right."

Anne couldn't have been more discouraged by Max's tone, especially when they had green lights on scope, schedule, and budget. She remembered when Max used to have a very positive attitude toward work. Now he arrived late and spent most of the day taking coffee breaks. Several project team members had recently complained to Anne about Max's sarcastic and cynical comments.

Max was a brilliant process engineer and certainly could not be easily replaced, if at all, but Anne felt that she had no choice. She scheduled an appointment with her project sponsor, a senior manufacturing executive, to discuss the situation.

These types of scenarios occur everyday across the world. As project leaders we need some framework for understanding what is blocking the motivation of our project team members. We have adapted a motivation framework from the expectancy theory work of Ed Lawler and Lyman Porter. We found in our work that this simple framework provides a tool for project leaders to understand what blocks team members from achieving high levels of performance. This model is depicted in Figure 6.2

This straightforward framework provides the opportunity to formulate three simple questions that will help us uncover what might be blocking an individual's motivation and performance. You can fill in the blank with a project team member with whom you may be experiencing some challenges.

1. If _____ exerts the appropriate amount of effort, s/he can achieve desired performance results.
   (Strongly Disagree   1   2   3   4   5   Strongly Agree)
2. If _____ achieves desired performance results, s/he is rewarded.
   (Strongly Disagree   1   2   3   4   5   Strongly Agree)
3. _____ believes the rewards are attractive.
   (Strongly Disagree   1   2   3   4   5   Strongly Agree)

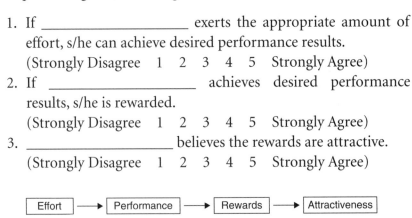

Figure 6.2 A Framework for Identifying What Blocks Motivation and Performance.

We have found that these three simple questions, if answered honestly, pinpoint motivation and performance problems with great accuracy. In the case of Max Hoffman, he was certainly able to perform if he put in the effort. He was a brilliant process engineer. Anne Bremicker complemented Max when he completed his work and provided positive feedback to Max's boss. The underlying problem was that Max did not value the reward of positive feedback from Anne.

In talking with Max during a project leadership seminar, we found that he was quite dissatisfied with his project work despite his reputation as someone who could get things done quickly and professionally. In fact, Max had the reputation of being one of the few people in the company with the skills required to perform certain types of value stream analysis. He routinely received top ratings in the annual review process for the company and project leaders essentially waited in line to have Max as a team member on their projects.

As Max put it, "I keep getting asked to do this type of value stream mapping. It's a very detailed and time-consuming process that I've mastered. The problem is that I don't want to do it anymore. I want to take on some new challenges, but I keep getting asked to do this work because I am one of the few who understand the intricacies of the analyses."

We see people like Max on a regular basis. These are the dissatisfied heroes of the project world. They are the individual contributors who deliver consistent results. These are the people that we call on when we need to get something done. Max ended up leaving the company to pursue opportunities for growth. We learn from Max's situation that we need to do reality checks to ensure that the WIIFM aspects of the project vision truly resonate with our stakeholders.

Max's functional manager and the project leaders in the organization had no idea that Max was getting burnt out by continuing to do so much value stream mapping. He needed a new opportunity. As project leaders, we need to pause periodically to better understand what project team members really need from us.

Imperative 5

As project leaders, we need to pause periodically to better understand what project team members really need from us. The Effort–Performance–Rewards–Attractiveness model helps us understand what might be blocking motivation and performance.

In this next scenario, we find Marcus Eriksson, an IT subject matter expert, floundering while the project leader seems to be unaware of the predicament.

The Hands-Off Project Leader

Marcus Eriksson sat in his office sharing his predicament with his colleague, Ana Grinsted. "I just don't know how to tell Hans that I don't have the skills needed to develop the software that he needs for this project. He encouraged me to participate on the Excalibur project because he heard that I performed so well on the XML integration project for the SAP implementation in Spain. But this Web portal development stuff is way beyond my capabilities."

Ana couldn't believe that Marcus would put the Excalibur project in jeopardy over his own insecurities. Why wouldn't he just tell Hans Jansen, the Excalibur project leader, that he needed help? He should have been working on this for the past month. That means we're potentially a month behind schedule, and we only launched this project 3 months ago.

As Hans Jansen chatted with other IT project leaders over lunch, he raised the issue of his concern about possibly being too hands-off in his leadership style. "I really didn't have much of a kickoff meeting with the project team. It's probably OK since the project team is made up of highly skilled IT professionals who have done this kind of work before. I've met with most of them individually, and I haven't backed off on the e-mail traffic at all. They have all the documents with respect to project scope and schedule requirements. Probably best to just trust that they will do the job and avoid micromanaging them, but I'm beginning to wonder if Marcus is placing this project as a priority. Come to think of it, I wonder how the business process standardization team members are doing...."

In this age of empowerment, some project leaders have gone too far. Clearly, Hans Jansen needs to get in touch with his project team members. Marcus doesn't want to disappoint Hans with the realization that he doesn't know how to develop the Web portal. As long as Marcus doesn't have the basic ability to do the work, effort will not lead to results. Hans needs to either find a way to increase the abilities of Marcus in a hurry or get another person on the team. We need to understand if our team members have the abilities that will allow them to achieve desired results if they put in the effort. In order to achieve this level of understanding, we must make ourselves available and listen to our project team members.

Imperative 6

LISTEN to everyone. "Bad news does not improve with age."

Consider another case that involves a marketing project leader, Anita Gupta, trying to get some information from a manufacturing engineer, Gabriel Ramirez. How many times do scenarios like this play out in projects within your organization?

Manufacturing Is from Mars; Marketing Is from Venus

Gabriel Ramirez sat in his cubicle shaking his head after his brief encounter with Anita Gupta, a project leader from marketing, who was asking for details about the production capacity for a new aspirin/calcium caplet. It was the first time she'd asked for these details, but she made it clear that if she didn't have the information by the end of the week she would be talking to the supply chain group head, a couple levels up the organization from Gabriel.

Earlier that week, Gabriel's boss assigned a new set of priorities that did not include Gupta's analysis. Aside from these new priorities within his own department, Gabriel had project work to complete for several other project leaders.

In hallway conversation with one of the other manufacturing engineers, Gabriel stated, "I just don't get it. These project leaders march in here like they own my world, as if we don't have anything else to do but work on their projects. The marketing project leaders tend to be the worst. They don't have a clue what it takes to deliver the goods. They seem to make promises that they can't back up, and we pay the price."

In the meantime, Anita Gupta was having a conversation with one of her marketing colleagues. "It's as if I was asking Ramirez for some personal favor. I can tell he doesn't like me. He said he would *try* to get the data that I needed. Trying just isn't good enough. 'Trying' usually means that it really won't happen. I told Gabriel that I would go to the supply chain head, Jim Peterson, if he couldn't get the data to me by the end of the week. It's too bad that it usually takes threats to get anything done on my project, but my job is on the line and I have to push hard to get products launched."

In addition to simply not liking Gupta, Ramirez cannot see how gathering the data for Gupta's report will improve his life in any way. Gupta's work is not part of his list of priorities. She's relying on an old-style management approach – "If you do as I ask, I will take my foot off your chest." In fact, if he takes the time to do her work he will take time away from the work that he needs to get done for his own boss.

Clearly, Gupta failed to display any empathy whatsoever for Gabriel's situation. She was focused singularly on what she wanted and needed rather than on how her needs impacted Ramirez. Simply communicating an understanding of Gabriel's situation would have gone a long way toward getting Gabriel to spend a bit of extra time to gather the data for the report. Additionally, Gupta could communicate with Gabriel's boss to try to get Gabriel's priorities better aligned with her own.

Imperative 7

Show empathy. Demonstrate that you can "put yourself in another's shoes."

Dealing with "Interesting" People

In one of our seminars, we raised the challenge of dealing with particularly difficult people. One of the participants told us, "We don't like to use the term difficult people. We like to consider them to be interesting people." After some reflection, we believe that it makes sense to use the "interesting" label. After all, Ritz-Carlton employees refer to customer problems as opportunities. They believe that recovering from service problems provide an opportunity to retain a customer for life. Similarly, uncovering what blocks the motivation of an "interesting" project team member provides an opportunity for project and career contributions.

As we stated in Chapter 1, Shackleton kept the troublemakers close. Similarly, we believe that we need to keep the interesting project team members close to us. Only then can we understand what blocks their motivation and performance. Before we spend too much effort on interesting project team members, we do need to assess whether or not they possess the basic capabilities that we need. Again, what we need should be dictated by the project scope. Do these project team members have what it takes to do the work that will lead to successful completion of the scope within schedule and budget constraints?

Imperative 8

Keep the "interesting" team members close. Spend the time to understand what is blocking their motivation and performance.

The Effort–Performance–Rewards–Attractiveness framework applies equally well to "interesting" project team members. The challenge in applying this framework to interesting project team members is that we need to overcome our tendency to simply write them off as unworthy. When we encounter someone like Max, our tendency is often to simply discount the person as someone with a bad attitude. If we have an HR policy that allows us to quickly change out team members and replace them with highly motivated ones, it may not be worth our time as project leaders to deal with the more challenging, or interesting, team members. However, most of us don't even have the luxury of selecting our team members much less replacing them unless there is compelling evidence that they do not have the skill set required to perform the project work.

Persistence and Optimism

Project leaders are special people. They are the ones who ensure that deliverables are achieved subject to budget and schedule constraints. More often than not, global project leaders have immense responsibility and little or no formal authority. They have to influence diverse and geographically distributed stakeholders to support the project.

Perhaps the most significant contribution a project leader can make to her team is to demonstrate persistence and optimism. Imagine the reverse – working for a project leader who makes statements such as "I don't think we're going to be able to make it." or "This is impossible. I can't believe leadership thinks we will be able to achieve these objectives." Project team members look to us as project leaders for cues. They watch us all the time. They not only listen to our words but they also read our body language.

Perhaps one of the greatest demonstrations of persistence and optimism comes from a speech given by Dr. Martin Luther King on August 23, 1963, on the steps of the Lincoln Memorial in Washington, DC. If we were to view King as a project leader, the ultimate deliverables of his project were freedom and equality. Here is a brief excerpt from the ending of his speech.

Let freedom ring from the snowcapped Rockies of Colorado!
Let freedom ring from the curvaceous slopes of California!
But not only that; let freedom ring from Stone Mountain of Georgia! Let freedom ring from Lookout Mountain of Tennessee! Let freedom ring from every hill and molehill of Mississippi. From every mountainside, let freedom ring. And when this happens, When we allow freedom to ring, when we let it ring from every village and every hamlet, from every state and every city, we will be able to speed up that day when all of God's children, black men and white men, Jews and Gentiles, Protestants and Catholics, will be able to join hands and sing in the words of the old Negro spiritual,
"Free at last! Free at last! Thank God Almighty, we are free at last!"

Martin Luther King personified optimism and persistence and paid the ultimate price for his steadfastness. He believed in what he was doing and he spread his persistence and optimism to others. We believe that we can learn from the steadfast optimism and persistence of great leaders like Martin Luther King to develop our own approaches for demonstrating passionate optimism and persistence.

Imperative 9

Demonstrate persistence and optimism.

Increasingly, we have to demonstrate persistence, listen, demonstrate empathy, and use other approaches to motivate team members that are not physically co-located. Virtual, or geographically distributed, project teams present unique challenges to us as project leaders.

What Virtual Project Team Members Need

We have found that the approaches that we've outlined in this chapter apply to virtual teams, but we need to recognize the constraint that project team members are not co-located. It's not unusual to find project team leaders managing projects that involve team members on multiple continents. Furthermore, we have found that many project leaders have not even met any of their team members.

Some of our discoveries may seem a bit counterintuitive at first. However, if you put yourself in the shoes of a project team member who might be working out of his house in a different country, the findings make a great deal of sense.

- Virtual project team members need to feel even more strongly connected to the purpose of the project than co-located team members.
- Virtual project team members need more, not less, interaction with project team members and project team leaders.
- Virtual project team members need to find ways to acquire skills and knowledge that they would otherwise acquire from working with others in close proximity.
- Virtual project team members need to feel connected to the purpose of the overall organization.

When the notion of virtual teams evolved, many envisioned independent people working remotely via the Internet and telecommunications. Somehow, many of us expected that a new breed of "virtual" people would emerge to fulfill the missions of geographically dispersed teams. This has not happened. People are people. The more remote we are, the more remote we feel.

What we have generally found is that virtual team members require more attention, not less. Technology makes them feel isolated, not connected. Therefore, what we need to give virtual team members is a feeling of connectedness. We need to spend extra time on the telephone, not just e-mail, connecting with virtual team members to make them feel valued and informed.

Imperative 10

Virtual project team members need more from us, not less.

Summary

We can have wonderful systems in place for planning the scope, schedule, and budget of projects. Web-based project tracking systems can provide us with a project dashboard to control projects with great precision. But at the end of the day, people make the difference. Project team members need to first have the skills required to perform the work of our projects but then they also have to be able to see that they are provided with some rewards that they find attractive.

We have provided a simple framework for understanding what might block motivation and performance. Additionally, we provided several scenarios to help understand how we can apply this framework. Finally, we provided ten imperatives to help guide our thinking around what project team members need from us as project leaders.

We encourage you to apply the framework and imperatives presented in this chapter. Truly understanding what project team members need from us, and ensuring that we have looked through their lenses to obtain this understanding, will separate us as global project leaders from those who simply manage projects.

What Team Members Need from Us – Imperatives

1. Whenever you can, make your teams as diverse as possible – diversity in male/female, in national cultures, in functions and in technical skills. Celebrate the ideas and results that come from this diversity.

2. Project team members needs evolve over the life of the project. If we recognize this, we can plan for changing needs and allow for shared leadership.

3. Recognize project team members for their positive behaviors. This simple process of recognition produces a lengthy stream of performance dividends.

4. Ask and then answer the "What's in it for me?" question from the perspective of each team member from his or her cultural lens.

5. As project leaders, we need to pause periodically to better understand what project team members really need from us. The Effort–Performance–Rewards–Attractiveness model helps us understand what might be blocking motivation and performance.

6. LISTEN to everyone as "Bad news does not improve with age."

7. Show empathy. Demonstrate that you can "put yourself in another's shoes."

8. Keep the "interesting" team members close. Spend the time to understand what is blocking their motivation and performance.

9. Demonstrate persistence and optimism.

10. Virtual project team members need more from us, not less.

7

Leading Projects at the Edge of Chaos

In this chapter, we share some approaches for leading projects at the edge of chaos, the fine line between order and disorder. We address the reality that the highly systematic approaches of project management can break down when we apply pressures of uncertainty, complexity, and stretched resources. Some of our approaches for leading projects at the edge of chaos are borrowed from the world of information technology project management, more specifically the world of agile project management. Other approaches come from lateral thinking, structured techniques for identifying both intended and unintended consequences in complex global projects. Ultimately, one of the strongest approaches for dealing with complexity is to simplify. We define simplicity as the art of deciding what you don't have to do and then committing to not doing it. Implementing this type of simplicity is somehow not so simple for most organizations.

To say that the world is becoming more complex, although certainly true, would overly simplify the challenges facing those who lead global projects. We find ourselves leading projects that have "fuzzy" or uncertain front ends and often feel as though we are making things up as we discuss next steps. Most of us don't have the luxury of direct reports. We borrow team members from other functions or even contractors. Despite understanding the importance of face-to-face communication, we get slapped in the face with budgets and geographical constraints that often limit our ability to ever meet our team members face-to-face. As we try to keep teams focused on the deliverables of a project, the deliverables often change based on shifting strategies and initiatives. We deal with uncertainties related to technologies, economies, companies, teams, and individuals to somehow fight against the tendency for things to simply fall apart.

An IT project leader related to us his frustration with traditional project management education. "We learned about scope, schedule, budgets, and risk management. Sure, I can put together a project plan and identify the critical path of a project. I can even perform earned value analysis to tell you how we are doing with respect to schedule and budget. The problem with this project management approach is that it assumes that somehow we control all events.

We don't. It's not like we are playing golf and we can simply adjust our swing. It's more like football (soccer in the United States). We have to anticipate the moves of our team members and the competition. Predicting exactly what's going to happen at a certain point in a football game is impossible. Adapting to circumstances can be much more important than having a perfect project plan."

This tension between planning and control on one side and adaptability on the other highlights the problem that many executives have with project management. Project management is often viewed as the burdensome set of shackles placed on an executive's initiative or project. We do not in any way discount the importance of project management. In fact, we have seen too many projects fail because accidental project managers thrust into the realm of leading major initiatives lack basic understanding of project management. Planning is a fundamental starting point. As the saying goes, "Failing to plan is planning to fail." But failing to adapt and pull the project pieces together based on current realities rather than initial assumptions and project plans is the kiss of death for many projects and initiatives.

Consider the case of a senior VP at a telecommunications company who decided to combat complexity and the challenges of rapid growth by implementing a project management office, or PMO. He was pressed to expand his fiber optics networks. Routing fiber optics to a particular customer involved cross-functional cooperation from several different technical groups within the organization as well as subcontracting organizations. Deep technical and organizational know-how existed within his organization and the contractors, but orchestrating each fiber optics installation was a project in and of itself. With hundreds of existing installations not meeting their targeted time frames of approximately 30 days, the executive decided to implement a PMO. He hired an outsider with deep project management experience and a widely recognized certification to head the PMO. The new PMO head hired people like himself, certified project managers who understood all phases of project planning, and execution as well as closing of contracts and projects.

The project managers drafted project plans with well-defined milestones and deliverables but performance on the fiber optics installations declined. The vice president who had established the PMO realized quickly that the structure imposed by the project managers was readily rejected by the people doing the actual work. The functional managers complained that the project managers were out of touch with the rapidly changing realities. The technical experts within the company and the contracting organizations had well-established ways of working together. The project management structure, at least to them, was getting in the way. The people who actually had to get the work done accused the project managers of slowing them down with reports and meetings that did not reflect the reality of what was happening on the ground. "If the PMs would just get out of our way, we could get our work done."

This telecommunications organization was scrambling to keep up with growth. It was adding new contractors and new employees. The organization's ability to meet its growth targets tipped closer to the edge of chaos when it pushed too hard with formal project management. Informal networks among technical experts and individuals in the supplier organizations were the glue that had held the resource stretched division of the telecommunications company together prior to the attempts to form a functioning PMO. The all-or-nothing imposition of project management caused a great deal of frustration. It was us (those doing the work) against them (the project managers who were getting in our way). We have found time and time again that applying by-the-book project management in its full force can hinder the progress of projects when an organization is facing a great deal of complexity, uncertainty, and other triggers that could tip projects into chaos.

Edge of Chaos Reality 1

Formal project management imposed in full force can impede the progress of organizations at the edge of chaos.

At some point, we find ourselves leading initiatives and projects at the edge of chaos. We cannot provide an absolute checklist for leading such projects. We can only share a composite of approaches that we have seen working in various organizations. The first step toward leading effectively under extreme conditions is to understand what is meant by the edge of chaos.

Understanding Chaos

Chaos is the antithesis of project management. With project management, we strive for order. Our project plans include scope, schedule, and budget baselines that we manage systematically to ensure that our actual performance does not vary significantly from plant performance. When we do we have variances, these variances are explained and adjustments are made. Control. Control. Control. It's what project managers do.

When a project slips into chaos, it enters a state of disorder and confusion. As global project leaders, we have to be looking for the inflection points at which order is lost and confusion reigns. Disorder and confusion at any particular point in our project can result in an overall sense of chaos. Generally speaking, most complex and long-duration projects tip from order and certainty into disorder and confusion many times over the lifecycle of the project. The magnitude of the chaos and our ability to drive the project back to some sense of order and clarity determines how much damage chaos will cause.

Most of us understand at a gut level the notion of a project being in chaos. The following comments were made by a Web programmer who had to change his plans to take a day off.

And then the project from hell comes raining down. You know, the one where things have been spinning further and further out of control for months, where the people who were working on it and had some idea of what it was supposed to do are gone, where the scope has gone entirely out the window, where your management is just cutting bait so the project doesn't continue as a black hole for money and time.[1]

---

[1]Web blog entry found at cwinters.com on August 8, 2007.

We encounter many frustrated project leaders in our work in helping organizations develop project leadership capabilities. Most of their frustration comes from feelings that they have somehow lost control of their projects, or taken to an extreme that they have never had control at all. They make comments like the one above from the Web programmer or simply tell us that events are changing so quickly that control is impossible to maintain.

When we dig deeper, we usually find that disorder and confusion exists in pockets within the project. We don't find many completely disordered projects in which all team members and stakeholders are confused. More often than not, we find that small but chaotic pockets of activities within projects cause great damage. As leaders of initiatives and projects, we need to be scanning for potential pockets of chaos that might keep us from achieving our deliverables, schedule, and budget objectives. It only takes one small crisis in a project to cause great damage. It's not likely to find too many projects in an organization that could actually be considered to be in chaos. But when we scan projects in most organizations, we can find pieces of many projects approaching or already in chaos.

The Airbus A380, mentioned briefly in Chapter 2, stands out as an example in which, at least for a period of time, a pocket of chaos caused significant damage. This highly complex global project tipped into crisis largely due to an inability to put together pieces of work from different global teams. Issues related at least partly to translating designs from geographically distributed teams into workable production plans led to costly overruns and delays in delivering the aircraft to both cargo and passenger carriers.

The A380 project represents a hallmark in aviation engineering. In December 2000, Airbus began an ambitious €8.8 billion project to build the world's largest passenger aircraft. The double-decker aircraft would carry 525 passengers across three classes of flight or up to 853 passengers if configured for only economy seats. For Airbus and its parent company EADS, the project was a big gamble. It was betting on a "bigger is better" strategy while its competitor Boeing was revising its fleet of long-haul aircraft in a more incremental fashion.

The A380 included 530 km of cables that required over 100,000 wires and 40,300 connectors. Integrating the designs of engineers in

Germany, Spain, France, and the United Kingdom proved to be more difficult than assumed. Ideally, the 3D computer-aided design software used by each team would have fed all updates to the final assembly operations in Toulouse, France. Ultimately, it was determined that the French and British design teams were using an upgraded computer-aided design software package whereas the German and Spanish teams were using a different version of the same software.[2] Due to system interoperability problems, some engineering updates did not automatically update in the 3D rendering of the design used for final production in Toulouse. Fixing this issue and many other smaller problems resulted in significant project delays.

The delays increased the costs of the overall project. This meant that more aircraft would have to be sold in order to cover the costs of development. To make matters worse, the company was forced to pay Singapore Airlines an undisclosed amount for enduring the production delays. FedEx and UPS canceled their orders to avoid the business impacts of further delays.

A small pocket of chaos resulting from interoperability issues with the design software tipped the A380 project, and arguably the company, into crisis. The delays resulted in significant lost operating profits. Whether or not the company will recover fully from the losses and achieve a positive return on the A380 project has yet to be determined as of the writing of this book. This type of problem, failing to integrate the pieces of a complex global project, is not uncommon. Neither is running with a basic assumption (the system will work) and finding out that the assumption was a critical and preventable risk to the project.

Edge of Chaos Reality 2

A small pocket of chaos can inflict tremendous damage.

Given this second reality, we cannot seek comfort in a general sense that a project is in control. We need to look for pockets of chaos, parts of our project characterized by high levels of disorder

[2]"Lessons for All CAD Users from the Airbus CATIA Debacle," by Randall S. Newton, AECnews.com, September 29, 2006.

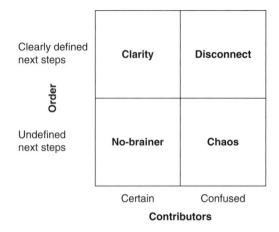

Figure 7.1   Looking for Chaos in Projects.

and confusion. We use this simple tool depicted in Figure 7.1 to help project leaders scanned for pockets of chaos in their projects.

We scan for chaos by looking at (1) whether or not next steps are identified and shared and (2) whether or not individual contributors are confused about what to do next. Depending on how critical a project might be for an organization, we take the analysis down to a rather granular level. For example, for a European financial services organization implementing an offshoring project in India, we would want to talk with teams in both Europe and India to assess the extent to which next steps are defined and the extent to which individual contributors are certain or confused about what to do next.

When project team members are confused about what to do next and we don't find any evidence of defined next steps, we flag this point in the project as a pocket of chaos. To be clear, definition of the next steps does not have to come from the project leader. It can, and in many cases should, come from the project team. But when we find that the team is confused and cannot come up with a list of next steps, we raise the "pocket of chaos" flag.

When people aren't sure about what they should be doing next, it's easy for them to switch to some other activity. We cannot count on clairvoyance. This is especially true for complex projects involving multiple handoffs between functions and even across external organizations. When we are handing off work without clear direction regarding next steps or receiving work with the same lack of clarity, it's unlikely that productive work will get done. Aside from general lack of control and lack of clarity, it's pretty common to see conflict over sources of confusion. We find a lot of blaming takes place when people are not clear about what they should be doing next. At this point of confusion about next steps, we must do whatever is necessary to get the project back to a state of clarity in which project contributors are clear about well-defined next steps. Specific approaches for achieving clarity will be shared later in this chapter.

When project team members are confused about what to do next with the steps are well defined in the project plan, we label this piece of the project as a Disconnect. Disconnects occur most often when the project planning and control system is not mirroring the reality of the project. This is what happened in the previous example in which the telecommunications vice president realized that the PMO was disconnected from the realities of the work being done. When we find these types of disconnects, we have to either get our project managers more connected with the reality of the business or consider abandoning highly structured project management approaches in favor of other approaches such as value stream mapping to streamline repeatable processes. Project management is not always appropriate for short-cycle repeatable types of work.

No-Brainers are the flip sides of Disconnects. Team members are instinctively certain about what to do next even when there is no formal project plan providing detailed documentation of next steps to be performed. These pieces of work probably do not merit extensive and formal project management. Checklists and documentation of best practices should be implemented in order to ensure that a no-brainer for an experienced employee will also be a no-brainer for a new hire.

The telecommunications vice president in our example decided to abandon highly structured project management approaches in favor of value stream mapping. He found that most of the fiber optics installations were highly repeatable short-cycle projects that simply needed to be streamlined by the multifunctional installation teams. A focus on waste reduction and repeatable best practices helped his organization move toward greater clarity in fiber optics installations. The emphasis was placed on how to best work together to reduce as many nonvalue-added steps as possible in order to meet customers' delivery objectives. This intersection of well-defined order with respect to next steps and certainty in the minds of individual contributors leads to clarity that enables progress.

Complexity and Uncertainty

Those leading highly complex projects often view clarity as an elusive concept. When thousands of potential small events, decisions, and assumptions can lead to untold unintended consequences, predicting exactly what has to be done proves to be an insurmountable challenge in many projects. Complexity is a big contributor to chaos. Add uncertainty, and pockets of chaos can be very difficult to avoid, especially in large and long-duration complex projects.

Chaos theory suggests that the starting point, or initial conditions, of the system can lead to complex and unpredictable results. The Butterfly Effect is often used to illustrate this phenomenon. If a butterfly beats its wings in China, the beating of the wings could affect weather patterns in Europe and North America. Large complex projects, especially long-duration ones, provide numerous opportunities for butterfly effects.

Edge of Chaos Reality 3

Seemingly inconsequential initial conditions can lead to complex and unpredictable project outcomes.

Consider again the Airbus A380 example. The starting point for the design teams was a computer-aided design systems operating with different versions. Nobody predicted the series of events that would unfold as a result of interoperability issues resulting from the different versions of the computer-aided design software. When complex wire harnesses didn't quite reach each other during the production process, one can be certain that those doing the production work were confused and uncertain about next steps, a pocket of chaos in an otherwise highly structured aerospace project.

Complexity theory differs from chaos theory primarily with respect to outcomes. Whereas chaos theory suggests that simple beginnings can lead to complex outcomes, complexity theory suggests that complex beginnings can lead to ordered outcomes. Whether we are talking about the biological origins of complexity theory or a complex project in which teams need to work together across functions and organizations, organizing mechanisms emerge to bring order complexly.

As individuals, we seek order by inventing our own processes to deal with complexity of our chaotic professional lives. We devise personal strategies such as filtering our carbon copy e-mails to separate folders to give us the time to first address the e-mails for which we are the primary addressee. We schedule meetings with ourselves to allow time for thinking and planning. Just as we might each develop our own personal coping mechanisms, as leaders of global projects we have to consider organizational coping mechanisms.

Formal project management approaches such as project planning, control, and risk management seek order at an organizational level. Many organizations such as integrated oil and gas companies obtain excellent results through highly structured project management systems. They have years of experience in dealing with the complexity of oil and gas exploration, production, and distribution. This experience can be translated into highly structured project management approaches to manage hugely complex capital projects that often have price tags in the billions USD. But when similar projects have not been done in the past, we often face both complexity and uncertainty.

Complex projects are often burdened with the added baggage of uncertainty. Large-scale the IT industry provides uncountable examples of both complex and uncertain projects. In many IT projects, technology evolves so quickly that it becomes nearly impossible to predict with certainty what tasks will need to be performed in the long run. Web portal design or early installations of enterprise resource planning systems provide classic examples of projects that are both complex and involve a great deal of uncertainty. But we do not have to look to the IT industry for complex and uncertain projects. Projects aimed at organizational changes such as increasing cross-functional sharing of best practices on a global basis provide ample complexity and uncertainty.

When asked about complexity and uncertainty, the head of development for a global pharmaceutical company stated, "We ask our project managers to walk into the unknown." Despite the methodical approach to project management that might be implied by basic project management software and the highly structured approach taught in many project management fundamentals classes, we believe that project leadership for complex global projects is not so much about managing the known. We are not simply laying out a work breakdown chart, project schedule, and budget based on clearly identified scope. Fundamental project planning and risk management tools, while very important, are not sufficient for leading projects at the edge of chaos. We need to turn to new approaches to avoid pockets of chaos and ensure project clarity.

In Figure 7.1, we provided the big picture of how to identify pockets of chaos in projects. We look for points at which next steps are unclear and individual contributors are confused. This simple model provides a radar screen that we can use to search for potential pockets of chaos. Sophisticated leaders of global initiatives and projects also need to be on alert for specific early warning signs that could indicate the potential for chaos.

Early Warning Signs

We have the opportunity to interact with hundreds of project leaders each year and hear litanies about projects that have reached a state of chaos. These project leaders are unclear about what to do next and their team members are confused. We know that complex and uncertain projects are more likely to slip into chaos than

Table 7.1   Project Chaos Early Warning Signs

- Expressed confusion about the strategy that the project is fulfilling
- Real or perceived confusion about the project scope
- Project team members focusing on work unrelated to the project
- Isolated virtual team members
- Stuck in the glue of a fuzzy front end

straightforward predictable projects. We also have a pretty good idea of what chaos looks like, but identifying early warning signs can be more challenging. We have identified numerous conditions that individually or collectively can lead to project chaos. Surely, this is a partial list. If we were to dig even deeper we could likely identify hundreds of potential inflection points at which next steps become unclear and/or individual contributors become confused. Additionally, the early warning signs, summarized in Table 7.1, that we have identified in our interactions with project leaders might differ from some of the early warning signs specific to your organization. Part of our advice on dealing with early warning signs is to develop your own list based on your experience and the collective wisdom of your peers and project team members.

Edge of Chaos Reality 4

We can identify early warning signs to avoid pockets of chaos.

Expressed Confusion About the Strategy That the Project is Fulfilling

Projects are strategy in motion. If we are unclear on the overall organizational or business strategy or we allow that strategy to blow in the breeze, confusion will exist about why we are pursuing a project. Any efforts to control a project are quickly offset by the "Who cares?" factor. If we are unclear about why we are pursuing a project, it's difficult to get people excited about fitting the project work into their very busy schedules. Projects without clear purpose tend to be neglected. Neglected projects eventually enter the realm of chaos if they are not killed or provided with greater purpose before that point.

Real or Perceived Confusion About the Project Scope

Scope drives schedule, resources, and budget. If we jump into a project with lack of clarity about our deliverables or allow our project scope to change frequently without clearly controlling the impact of the changes, we set ourselves up for chaos. Not only are people unclear about next steps, but they lose motivation for the project work since they have too often been asked to redo their work based on changing project deliverables.

Our project scope might be well documented in a project plan, but individual team members need to be clear about the plan. In interventions with dysfunctional project teams, we continue to be amazed by the frequency with which scope can be well documented but not shared with project team members. Once you are clear on the scope, share this clarity with others.

Project Team Members Focusing on Work Unrelated to the Project

In some respects, focusing on work unrelated to the project might mean that the project is already in a state of chaos. But we have found that this simple barometer can be very effective as an early warning sign. When we ask project team members why they are not working on a particular project, their response is often that they simply don't know what they were supposed to do next so they are shifting their attention to a project with greater order and clarity. Other times they are not clear on why the project is being done. The physical manifestation of being unclear about next steps or the strategy which the project supports can be as simple as working on something other than the project.

If enough people who should be doing your project work are shying away from your work in favor of functional work or some other project work, interdependencies breakdown and controlling the project becomes difficult at best. But jumping to the conclusion that project team members are shirking responsibilities or suffer from too many competing priorities can be a mistake. It's possible that they are simply confused about the purpose of the project or next steps. They are in a small pocket of chaos.

Isolated Virtual Team Members

We found many instances when geographically distributed team members who were expected to rely primarily on e-mail eventually fell off the project grid. That is, these individual contributors drifted away from some of their projects. When we stop hearing from virtual team members, and we depend on them for getting project work done, there's a pretty good chance that project team members are confused and need direction.

Stuck in the Glue of a Fuzzy Front End

Many projects seek to commercialize some innovation. From the standpoint of managing projects, we define innovation as invention plus implementation. Invention alone is generally useless without translating the brilliance of the invention into commercialization, or in the case of nonprofit applications, simply putting new ideas to use. Innovation projects can be broken into three basic stages: the fuzzy front end, product development, and commercialization. Fuzzy front end subprojects within an overall product development cycle involve experimentation and assessment of many potential solutions that could be further developed and then commercialized. Depending on the industry, there can be a tremendous amount of uncertainty at these front ends. Oil exploration and pharmaceutical research stand out as examples of fuzzy front ends of large projects that could eventually reach commercialization.

In some cases, projects get stuck at the fuzzy front end. Research scientists can spend forever looking for a Eureka moment. We have spoken with pharmaceutical research scientists who have told us that nothing they have ever worked on has led to a commercialized product. This is not so unusual an industry in which thousands of compounds are researched for every one that makes it to an actual commercialized drug.

The problem with fuzzy front ends at the beginning of otherwise highly structured projects is that we get stuck too long in a cycle of not being able to predict the timing of next steps. Those waiting for the outputs of the fuzzy front end do not know when they will have to start next steps and in many cases don't know exactly what the next steps will be until the output of the front end process is complete.

In addition to these early warning signs, project leaders also have to be aware of the perfect storm of project management. We believe that the coming together of some basic "laws" of project management creates situations in which projects can be spun into crisis. By understanding early warning signs and the perfect storm of project management, we can take preventative and reactive measures to keep our project at the edge of chaos or, even better, in a state of clarity.

The Perfect Storm

The perfect storm of project management occurs at the intersection of three basic laws – Parkinson's Law, the Student Syndrome, and Murphy's Law. When this happens people allow too much time for a project task, they delay beginning the task, and they succumb to unpredictable disasters.

Parkinson's Law tells us that work expands to fill the allocated time. There are several consequences of this law. Most people tend to pad time estimates and then take the full amount of the estimated time, or more, to complete a task. When we visit their offices or cubicles to inquire about progress, we are often given the answer "I'm really working hard on this." We don't typically hear "I haven't given those tasks any thought at all." People remain busy even if very little work has actually been completed.

The Student Syndrome tells us that people, on average, will delay the start of activity. The term harkens back to term papers completed during the last few days or hours of a college term. Some individuals will complete work well ahead of time, but just as is the case with Parkinson's Law, we are talking about averages. On average, people procrastinate.

Murphy's Law tells us that if something can go wrong, it will go wrong. If we delay backing up our hard drive, it will crash. If we wait too long to prepare our presentation to the steering committee, the steering committee will suddenly ask us to present 2 days early. Again, some of us are lucky and have never experienced Murphy's Law. If you are among those lucky ones, congratulations. On average, Murphy's Law does hit us at the most unappreciated times during projects.

This perfect storm of project management is graphically displayed in Figure 7.2. When things go wrong near the end of the project it can be very difficult or impossible to recover in time to complete our project deliverables as promised. Assuming that our work feeds into the work of others, the project team can quickly lose clarity about next steps and become confused. The perfect storm can lead to pockets of chaos that cause delays and increase project cost.

When individuals or groups are working on tasks or work packages with very long durations, the impacts of the perfect storm become more pronounced. There are no early warning signs for the

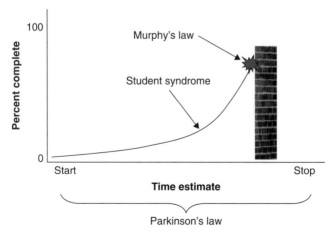

Figure 7.2   The Perfect Storm of Project Management.

perfect storm *per se* other than the nature of the tasks themselves. When we have a preponderance of long-duration tasks that feed into one another, the likelihood of the perfect storm causing pockets of chaos increases. Orchestrating multiple tasks feeding in from different project teams around the globe can be especially daunting when we are faced with the combined effects of Parkinson's Law, the Student Syndrome, and Murphy's Law.

Edge of Chaos Reality 5

The perfect storm of project management culminates in chaos.

We have identified numerous approaches that have helped project leaders to keep their projects somewhere between clarity and the edge of chaos as depicted in Figure 7.3. To suggest that a checklist of approaches could guarantee project clarity would ignore the reality based in organizations around the world. When our projects hit a pocket of chaos, we need to demonstrate our ability to lead our projects across the edge of chaos to clarity. When we achieve clarity, we need to find ways to maintain it.

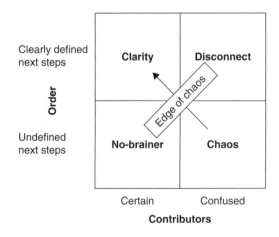

Figure 7.3   Pushing Across the Edge of Chaos to Clarity.

Table 7.2   Clarity-Seeking Approaches

- Identify and communicate project scope and the link between scope and strategy
- Carve long-duration projects and tasks into value-producing chunks
- Ask the critical three questions frequently, daily if possible
- Simplify
- Leverage diversity to achieve project breakthroughs
- Perform project team tune-ups on a regular basis
- Engage in lateral thinking to minimize assumptions and explore Butterfly Effects
- Structure your project by project type

Clarity-Seeking Project Leadership

Our job as project leaders is to help others find clarity in a complex and often uncertain world. We have identified several approaches, outlined in Table 7.2, to help us deal with the effects of complexity and uncertainty and prevent pockets of chaos. Each of the approaches that we share has been tested in practice. Some of the approaches are borrowed from the work of others. We do not hesitate to lean on others' good work as long as the ideas produce results. Several of the ideas in this section are adapted from the work of those involved in developing the Agile Manifesto[3] and Scrum[4] approaches developed primarily to deal with the complexity and uncertainty of IT projects.

Identify and Communicate Project Scope and the Link Between Scope and Strategy

This step should be fundamental to all projects, not just complex and uncertain ones. However, if a project is complex and uncertain more time needs to be spent scoping the project and making sense of how the project will contribute to overall strategy. As previously

---

[3]See http://www.agilemanifesto.org/principles.html
[4]For a description of scrum *see "Wicked Problems, Righteous Solutions: A Catolog of Modern Engineering Paradigms,"* by Peter DeGrace and Leslie Hulet Stahl, Prentice Hall, 1998.

stated, we all too often hear that project team members don't understand why they are working on a particular project. When confused about purpose, individual contributors often shift their attention elsewhere. At some point this confusion with respect to purpose combined with ignored work leads to great uncertainty about next steps. To avoid this pocket of chaos, spend the time necessary to make sure that all individual contributors are very clear about the scope of the project and how the project contributes to overall business and organizational strategy.

Carve Long-Duration Projects and Tasks into Value-Producing Chunks

One way to counterbalance the effects of the perfect storm of project management is to carve long-duration tasks and even projects into much shorter value-producing chunks.[5] If a phase of a project is estimated to take six months and requires the output of four functional areas and three suppliers, the likelihood of everything coming together as planned is limited at best. We have found in practice that identifying subprojects, or chunks, with standalone benefits decreases the negative impacts of Parkinson's Law, the Student Syndrome, and Murphy's Law.

By moving quickly and achieving standalone value from the output of a subproject, or chunk, project teams build momentum and the organization sees incremental value from the work. For example, if a complex implementation of a human resources management module within an enterprise resource planning system begins with simply integrating key talent information from across the globe into a data warehouse, executives can put this project chunk to use immediately.

---

[5]This notion of chunks and value-producing subprojects (or rapid results initiatives) has been highlighted in two Harvard Business Review articles: (1) *"Close the Gap Between Projects and Strategy,"* by Lauren Keller Johnson, June 1, 2004; (2) *"Why Good Projects Fail Anyway,"* by Nadim F. Matta and Ronald N. Ashkenas, September 1, 2003.

Ask the Critical Three Questions Frequently, Daily if Possible

These three questions, adapted closely from the work of Jeff Sutherland, a cofounder of the agile project management process called Scrum, probably do more to avoid chaos than any other approach.

1. What Have You Done Since the Last Meeting?

Sutherland and fellow "Scrum Masters" recommend frequent but brief meetings. Imagine the impact on your work if you know today that someone will be asking you tomorrow about what you have accomplished. From the project leader's perspective, the question provides a quick check that individual contributors understood next steps and were not confused. If somebody is in a pocket of chaos, it will be readily apparent to the project leader.

2. What Are the Barriers Getting in the Way of Your Progress?

The project leader needs to eliminate barriers to clarity and also any barriers to getting the actual work done. The barriers could be lack of focus from competing demands, processor technology problems, and a host of other factors that impede progress.

Another factor that often shows up as a barrier is the psychological state of the individual contributor. A leader of a geographically distributed project team encouraged the use of different smiley or sad faces in e-mail correspondence. These faces such as ☺, ☻, or ☹ at the bottom of an e-mail did not reflect the content of the e-mail or what a recipient thought of the original e-mail. Rather the faces represented the mood of the project team member. Sad faced e-mails would be followed up with a quick phone call from the project leader to identify what was wrong.

In addition to humanizing e-mail connections, the faces on the e-mail provided rapid feedback that some barrier existed in the project. We are not suggesting that little faces on e-mails should replace the simple question of what's getting in the way, but the faces do provide another mechanism for identifying any barriers that could tip project work into a pocket of chaos for a virtual team.

3. What Will You Accomplish Before Our Next Meeting?

By asking this simple question, any confusion or lack of clarity about next steps can be corrected immediately. We are not sitting by idly waiting for some of the early warning signs that we outlined earlier in the chapter.

It's worth noting that this third question and the first question are not building blocks for micromanagement. We are not dictating how the work should be done. We are merely connecting with individual contributors to ensure clarity. It is not surprising to see some initial pushback among project team members if this approach is used by generally hands-off project leaders. The second question softens the blow by emphasizing the coaching and facilitating role of the project leader. The overall message is that we are in this together to achieve agreed-upon objectives and we will work together to eliminate any barriers.

Simplify

Simplification is the art of identifying work that we don't need to do, and then committing to not doing it. If you just read that sentence quickly, read it again. Simplification is about figuring out what we *don't* have to do. Simplification is not about efficiency. We are not trying to cram more into our multitasked day. Rather, we focus on eliminating unnecessary meetings, reports, and other activities that do not contribute value to the successful completion of our project deliverables.

Most project leaders and team members that we work with are already sufficiently stressed. Our impression from working with a broad cross-section of organizations is that stress and multitasking are pushing many project leaders and contributors to the breaking point. Simplification should be a sanity-seeking approach. Too much stress hurts performance. Simplification can help project stakeholders focus on the project through greater clarity combined with increased capacity to get the work done. Selling simplicity as a means for piling on more work will only *increase stress and decrease commitment to simplification.* Simplicity increases and focus.

Leverage Diversity to Achieve Project Breakthroughs

Our functional and cultural paradigms often blind us to new ideas. Although we can have some really good ideas within a function or as a group of Europeans or Americans or Asians, the sparks of break-throughs will more likely occur when people with different views of the world are put together. When marketers and development people talk with one another, breakthroughs in how to start some product launch activities in parallel with development work can lead to early launches and huge increases in revenue. When IT people interact authentically with the business side of the house, new possibilities about how to reengineer processes to increase speed and value delivery emerge.

When we deliver project leadership training within corporations, we encourage the organizations to mix the group of participants by both function and culture. The sharing of ideas among diverse program participants creates multiplier effects well beyond the learning from any particular program content. Similarly, project leaders need to find ways to leverage diversity and even create some constructive conflict from time to time to encourage new ideas at the intersection of functional silos and country cultures. Collaboration increases clarity and keeps us out of pockets of chaos that can occur the intersections of different paradigms. The best way to avoid confusion and next step is to collaborate with authenticity.

Perform Project Team Tune-Ups on a Regular Basis

Project teams are like families. Just as we may hold a family meeting on a weekly basis to discuss our needs and how we are treating one another, project meetings should be held regularly to discuss the same issues. In addition to our regular meetings in which we would ask the three questions, we like to hold less frequent meetings to discuss how we interact with each other and what can be done to improve the spirit and performance of the team.

One virtual team leader discovered that his project team members felt rather isolated within a few months of face-to-face team meetings. The team discussed various approaches that could be implemented to make the team members feel more connected over time. A very creative approach emerged. The team decided that photographs from the bowling event or special dinner would be released in stages with a few new photos being released every week. Team members looked forward to the new photo releases and felt more connected to the rest of the team. They often called each other after the photos were released and in the process of reminiscing shifted to discussing project tasks. This creative approach increased project clarity while also making the team members feel more connected on a personal level.

Engage in Lateral Thinking to Minimize Assumptions and Explore Butterfly Effects

Occam's razor, a term attributed to an English Franciscan friar and philosopher of the late 13th in early 14th century, can guide us in our quest for focusing on those things that truly matter when addressing complex situations. Simply stated, we should make as few assumptions as possible. This principle does not mean that we strive endlessly to achieve complete certainty. Rather, it means that we as project leaders must think more laterally than linearly about our projects. We need to map the project terrain so we don't find ourselves saying "I hadn't thought of ...." or "I assumed they were acting in our best interest...."

Mind mapping and other lateral thinking approaches can help us visualize multiple scenarios emanating from small starting points and assumptions. For example, we might assume that project teams from the United States and Canada would not encounter significant cultural barriers. However, if we branched out laterally from that assumption and dig deeply into the underpinning reasons for stating the assumption we might realize that significant cultural differences do exist and should be acknowledged.

Assumptions about how we will work together, the disposition of stakeholders, the integration of technology, and the ability of different functions to pull together their work into a finished product are but a few examples that could be subjected to broader lateral thinking to ensure that the assumptions are not the beginning of a Butterfly Effect that could lead to pockets of chaos within our project. We need to map the project terrain as broadly as possible using mind mapping and brainstorming types of approaches to consider and then prevent many potential paths of assumptions and actions that could lead to chaos.

By its very nature, it's impossible to understand all of the potential causes of chaos. We have focused on some common causes and common cures to avoid casting our net too wide. For example, a South Korean conglomerate changed CEOs. With this change came a shift from an orientation toward growth and investment toward an orientation focusing on cost containment and return on investment. Many projects were tipped into chaos as the strategy changed. These types of shifts in strategic direction can cause sweeping chaos since existing projects no longer support the new strategy. The reality of business is that sometimes we have to deal with big shifts in direction that do not lend themselves to straightforward prescriptions. Again, our attempt in this chapter was to share some emerging ideas that might help you keep pockets of chaos from occurring in your projects or help you steer out of project chaos.

Structure Your Project by Project Type

Inexperienced project managers fall into the trap of treating all projects as though they are the same. We have heard project managers say, "A project is a project. As long as I apply systematic project management practices, I can manage any project." We do not share this view. A list of several project types we encounter regularly is included in Table 7.3.

Table 7.3 Project Types

■ Product Development Projects
■ Organizational Change Projects
■ Process Optimization Projects
■ IT and Business Services Projects
■ Compliance Projects
■ Research Projects
■ Capital Improvement Projects
■ Product Launch Projects

Managing each of these project types in a uniform manner would not make sense. Each type of project requires different time frames, applications of technologies, subject matter expertise, levels of cross-functional involvement, levels of coordination with external customers and suppliers, emphases on cost versus revenue, and numerous other points of divergence.

Applying construction project management approaches to research projects virtually guarantees failure. Researchers do not respond to the rigid project management structure required to construct a new building. We need to adapt our project management approaches to fit the unique circumstances associated with each project type. This does not invalidate the need to focus on the basics of scope, schedule, and budget. However, the extent to which we apply tight or loose controls and our faith in estimates and necessity for risk management will vary significantly across the range of project types displayed in Table 7.3

These clarity-seeking approaches have been adapted from agile project leadership techniques as well as best practices shared by practicing project leaders. Project leadership approaches, especially at the edge of chaos, require constant experimentation and reinvention. We do not advocate direct application of each bullet point in this or any other chapter. Rather, we offer approaches that we have seen work in practice and hope you will consider them as best practices that may support your project leadership needs.

Conclusion

Pockets of chaos occur when next steps are unclear and confusion prevails. Complexity and uncertainty are the fuel of project chaos. Long-duration projects and tasks often sail into the perfect storm of Parkinson's Law, the Student Syndrome, and Murphy's Law. As skillful leaders of global projects, we can read some of the early warning signs and adjust our course accordingly.

We provided several prescriptive actions for keeping our projects away from pockets of chaos. Perhaps one of the strongest prescriptions, coming from Scrum methodology, is the asking of three simple questions. By simply increasing frequency of contact with team members and focusing on progress to date, barriers, and next steps, project leaders can provide a great deal of clarity even in rapidly changing and uncertain environments.

The approaches that we have shared have been tested by project leaders and have demonstrated good results in improving project clarity. The techniques, like many prescriptions in this book, are intentionally simple. Simplicity is the best countermeasure to lead project team members through the sea of complexity and uncertainty. Clarity is the greatest gift that we as project leaders can give to our team.

Edge of Chaos Realities

1. Formal project management imposed in full force can impede the progress of organizations at the edge of chaos.

2. A small pocket of chaos can inflict tremendous damage.

3. Seemingly inconsequential initial conditions can lead to complex and unpredictable project outcomes.

4. We can identify early warning signs to avoid pockets of chaos.

5. The perfect storm of project management culminates in chaos.

8

Shaking Up the Project Team

This chapter is about change, a powerful topic especially over the past 15 years during an era of globalization, mergers, alliances, acquisitions, upsizing, downsizing, and rightsizing. With change comes the necessity to make transitions, which have a personal, emotional, and intellectual impact on all.

Change Imperative 1

Change is everywhere.

Our 70 plus professional work years includes working in organizations or with people as diverse as:

- The Catholic Church
- US military
- Several academic institutions
- Not for profit enterprises
- High tech engineering firms
- Our families
- Coaching leaders of global project teams

In the Catholic Church about 45 years ago, one of the many changes was using the vernacular of the country instead of Latin in the liturgy. In academic institutions the changes involved curriculum modification and ways to compensate faculty. In high tech engineering enterprises, the changes involve merging with another engineering company, and in our families dealing with careers and children who are now adults. Change and often big change is probably here to stay.

Change Imperative 2

People don't like change.

We begin with these quotations.

If you want to change/transform anything or anybody, the best place to start is with yourself.

Source: Unknown

Start with a cage containing 5 monkeys. Inside the cage, hang a banana on a string and place a set of stairs under it. Before long, a monkey will go to the stairs and start to climb toward the banana. As soon as he touches the stairs, spray all of the other monkeys with cold water. After a while, another monkey makes an attempt with the same result – all the other monkeys are sprayed with cold water. Pretty soon, when another monkey tries to climb the stairs, the other monkeys will try to prevent it.

Now, put away the cold water. Remove one monkey from the cage and replace it with a new one. The new monkey sees the banana and wants to climb the stairs. To his surprise and horror, all the other monkeys attack him. After another attempt and attack, he knows that if he tries to climb the stairs, he will be assaulted. Next, remove another of the original five monkeys and replace it with a new one. The newcomer goes to the stairs and is attacked. The previous newcomer takes part in the punishment with enthusiasm! Likewise, replace a third original monkey with a new one, then a fourth, then a fifth. Every time the newest monkey takes to the stairs, he is attacked. Most of the monkeys that are beating him have no idea why they were not permitted to climb the stairs or why they are participating in the beating of the newest monkey. After replacing all the original monkeys, none of the remaining monkeys have ever been sprayed with cold water. Nevertheless, no monkey ever again approaches the stairs to try for the banana. Why not? Because as far as they know, that's the way it's always been done around here. And that, my friends, is how company policy begins.

Source: Unknown

Percy Barnevik, the former CEO of ABB, a global enterprise of a Swiss and Swedish company said:

I try to make people at ABB accept that change is a way of life. I often got the question from Swiss and Germans: "Mr. Barnevik, aren't you happy now? Can't we relax a bit?" They see new targets as a threat or an inconvenience. But I say you must get used to the idea that we are changing all the time.

Peter Drucker wrote about change this way in his book "Post Capitalist Society."

Every few years in Western history there occurs a sharp transformation ... a divide. Within a few short decades, society rearranges itself – its world view; its basic values; its social structure; its arts; its key institutions. Fifty years later, there is a new world. And the people born then cannot even imagine the world in which their grandparents lived and into which their own parents were born. We are currently living through just such a transformation.

Most scientist believe planet Earth has been in existence between three and four billion years. There have been mind boggling changes between the beginnings and about 100,000 years ago, when small numbers of modern humans left Africa and progressively colonized much of the rest of the world. In our own lifetime, the changes in medicine, in telecommunications, computers, science, air travel, and changes virtually everywhere are equally staggering. As parents and grandparents, we think about the future and wonder what will happen in the lifetimes of our children and their children. In Africa, we are concerned with hunger and disease. In many of the more affluent countries we worry about crime and the obesity of our children. Change is everywhere.

"Every time I meet with my team about important issues covering our projects I am, in a way, asking them to change."
A leader of a major project for a European pharmaceutical company

Change Imperative 3

Many change initiatives fail to reach their full potential.

Global organizations change as well. Samsung Semiconductor, which is the largest of Korean's Samsung Electronics division and one of the world's largest semiconductors makers tried to change managers from being "task masters" to a "coaching orientation."

Hewlett-Packard has been a respectable US global company for years. The HP way emphasized both people and profits. They acquired Compaq which resulted in a major change process for both companies.

IBM was in trouble when it hired Louis Gerstner as chairman and CEO. He brought the company together. Gerstner said:

> We needed to integrate as a team inside the company so that we could integrate for the customers on their premises. It flew in the face of what everybody did in their careers before I arrived there. It meant that we would share technical plans, we would move toward common technical standards and plans, we would not have individual transfer pricing between every product so that everybody could get their little piece of the customers' money.

Unilever, in the 1990s, told managers who were unaccustomed to radical change, they had to accept a new strategic approach or leave.

British Airways changed from "bloody awful" to "bloody awesome" through reorganization and a new corporate culture.

Peter Senge, one of the "gurus" on change and "learning organizations" believes that "most change initiatives fail to reach their potential." He refers to independent studies of Total Quality Management that found that the majority are stopped because they did not produce results. Reengineering studies found that the failure rate is about 70% and in a study of 100 "corporation transformation efforts more than half did not survive the initial phases."

Leaders of global projects can easily identify change initiatives in their organizations and in their project teams that failed to reach their potential. This can be shown in Figure 8.1.

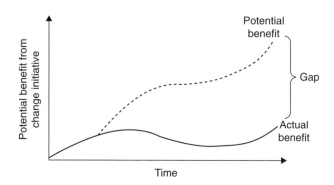

Figure 8.1   Benefit over time relationship. Modified from *The Dance of Change*, Peter Senge *et al.*, 1999

Why is this so? We believe the answer is simple. It is because change agents/leaders of global projects and others who are involved in change do not understand the individual or organizational change process. We believe if we had a few clear paradigms of change, some "tips" for leaders of change and some questions to ask during the various stages of the change process, all would become more skillful and the benefits over time would be more realized.

Change Imperative 4

Commit to understanding why change initiatives fail.

"If it ain't broke, don't fix it" … a key organizational issue in the past used to be stability, now it is change. Several years ago senior executives from Europe and North America met to discuss survival in this extremely competitive world. It was the executives' general consensus that the only survivors will be those who understand and manage change effectively.

Price Pritchett and Ron Pound in their short book *The Employee Handout for Organizational Change* outline some useful ideas on change that are applicable to leaders of global projects. They begin by challenging some myths.

Myth	Reality
It will go away	It won't
My job is the same	You need to change too
Problems prove that changes are harmful for the organization	Problems are part of the change process
I'm not in a position to make a difference	You are part of the solution or part of problem
They don't know what they are doing	Some mistakes are inevitable

They also make some recommendations about being a change agent.

- Be positive
- Take ownership of the changes
- Select your battles
- Be tolerant of mistakes
- Practice stress management

Jack Welsh, former CEO of General Electric said the following:

When I try to summarize what I've learned since 1981, one of the big lesson is that change has no constituency. People like the status quo. They like the way it was. When you start changing things, the good old days look better and better…You've got to be prepared for massive resistance. Incremental change doesn't work very well in the type of transformation GE has gone through. If your change isn't big enough, revolutionary enough, the bureaucracy can beat you.

"People like the status quo" … just like monkeys who do not approach the stairs for the banana because "that's the way it has always been done around here."

The Change Process

Senge outlines the three fundamental challenges in any change process namely, getting started, sustaining, and redesigning.

The Challenge of Initiating
1. There's not enough time
2. We don't have help
3. It's not relevant
4. They're not walking the talk

The Challenge of Sustaining
1. Fear and anxiety of individuals
2. Assessing and measuring if it works
3. Believers and skeptics

The Challenge of Redesigning and Rethinking
1. They won't give up power
2. We keep reinventing the wheel
3. Where are we going

Change Implementation Insights

Dr. Warren Wilhelm, a colleague who has worked with General Electric and understands well the GE model of change suggests the following factors to be considered carefully by leaders involved in changes. These relate to creating a "sense of ownership," which prepares people impacted by any change to prepare and accept.

Leaders of Global Projects Remember:
1. All organizational change equates to personal change.
2. The only ones who like change are babies with wet diapers.
3. Any change must be aligned with the scope or charter of the project.
4. Effective changes mean individuals have a clear understanding of future direction.
5. For people to change "a burning platform" helps.
6. People resist not change necessarily, but "how they are changed."

For lessons learned, Wilhelm also has these points for initiators of change.

- *What gets measured, gets done; what gets rewarded, stays.*
- *High levels of commitment are achieved through involvement.*
- *Roles and responsibilities must be clarified and reclarified throughout the change process.*
- *Steering committee input is important.*
- *Overcommunicating with key stakeholders is nearly impossible.*

Change Imperative 5

Organizational change equates to personal change.

Build your own paradigm or model of change – for success or for failure. We have so far suggested five imperatives regarding change and a number of lessons learned have been articulated. Now, we ask you to reflect on these and complete the following task.

Part 1

Think of a change process in a project that you are familiar with that you consider a FAILURE. Briefly describe the project and the change process.

_____

_____

_____

_____

_____

_____

_____

Part 2

List the two or three factors that you believe were associated with the failure.

Factor 1_____

_____

_____

Factor 2_____

_____

_____

Factor 3_____

_____

_____

Part 3

Now think of a change process in a project that you are familiar with that you consider a SUCCESS. Briefly describe the project and the change process.

_____

_____

_____

_____

_____

_____

_____

Part 4

List the two or three factors what you believe were associated with the SUCCESS.

Factor 1_____

_____

Factor 2_____

_____

Factor 3_____

_____

Part 5

Now build your paradigm/model of change that you will use when you lead global projects and need to initiate change.

My paradigm/model of change:

MODEL

```




```

In summary, I will avoid these behaviors.

1.
2.
3.

In summary, I will do more of these behaviors.

1.
2.
3.

Change Imperative 6

Change takes COURAGE.

We have an interesting speak-up mentality in our company. We speak up if we agree with the boss. If a difference of opinion is ever expressed it must be said very carefully.

Leader of a global project for a major global company.

How many times have we heard a CEO make a presentation to key people and at the beginning, during, or at the end of a presentation say, "I look forward to your questions and having a good dialogue" and then the CEO is disappointed. The hallway conversation, however, suggests there were many disagreements but they did not "speak up."

The individuals behaved in a way that they believed the CEO wanted them to behave (he or she really did not want any controversy at the meeting) and they did NOT share their ideas and opinions because they differed in part with the CEO's ideas.

Most of the big mistakes I have made in my professional career involve occasions when I did not have the courage to question, to challenge, or to suggest an alternative way.

A department head

The US space shuttle Challenger exploded in 1986 killing all on board. An investigation found a number of engineers had questioned the safety of the launch but their concerns were ignored by NASA because of a commitment to proceed and a fear of "speaking up."

Risk and courage are related. Read on.

Change Imperative 7

Change means risk.

We conclude with the following and ask readers to reflect on the words and then assess themselves on the continuum of risk.

To laugh is to risk appearing the fool.
To weep is to risk appearing sentimental.
To reach out for another is to risk involvement.
To expose feelings is to risk exposing your true self.
To place your ideas, your dreams before the crowd is to risk loss.
To love is to risk not being loved in return.
To live is to risk dying.
To hope is to risk despair.
To try is to risk failure.
But, risks must be taken because the greatest hazard in life is to risk nothing.
The person who risks nothing, does nothing, has nothing, is nothing.
He or she may avoid suffering and sorrow.
But he or she simply cannot learn, feel, change, grow, love–live.
Chained by his or her certitudes he or she is a slave.
He or she has forfeited freedom.
Only a person who risks is free.

Source: Unknown

Are you a risk taker? In general? Professionally? As a leader of global projects? In leisure/travel? In relationships?

Rate yourself on a scale of 1–5 and then reread the anonymous words on risk.

Low on risk taking			High on risk taking	
1	2	3	4	5

Change Imperatives

1. Change is everywhere.
2. People don't change.
3. Many change initiatives fail to reach potential.
4. Commit to understanding why change initiatives fail.
5. Organizational change equates to personal change.
6. Change takes courage.
7. Change means risk.

A change freeze is like a snowman: it is a myth and would melt if heat were applied.

Source: Unknown

If we do not reward change, we are rewarding the status quo.

Source: Unknown

9

Leadership/Culture/ Project Management: Capturing the Learnings

We begin the next to the last chapter with a quote, "Visions without actions are hallucinations."

Whatever we have learned, in any context, must be internalized in the learner and incorporated into the practices of the organization. Otherwise, it is no better than dreams, hallucinations, and waste.

Last year a colleague related the following incident to us. Our academic institution was conducting a distance learning program at the MBA level and she was part of the faculty team. Distance learning is increasingly becoming a part of the offerings of many MBA programs. This program was structured so that the first and last sessions were on-campus. All other sessions were broadcast live from the main campus to 20 different satellite university sites where from 10 to 40 students had registered for the class.

This faculty person was visiting one satellite site and entered the classroom during a broadcast from the main campus. The number of enrolled students was 24. She told us, "There was not one person in the classroom. A few students were in the halls. I do not know where the other students were but all were expected to be in the classroom." This is an egregious example of abuse and a missed opportunity to learn. Although in defense of the 34 students who were not in the class, our colleague did say that the professor the students were supposed to be listening to was "extremely boring and very repetitive."

Methods of Learning

In our leading global projects we used a variety of learning methods. We believe our goal as educators is to connect the learnings in our programs to the professional world of the participants. Their ability to apply these learnings once they return to work is of utmost importance. We think of ourselves as educators not as entertainers and approach each program with these objectives at all times.

As in most executive education programs and virtually all MBA degree programs case studies are widely used. These case studies are usually written by faculty, and typically are available in a case study clearinghouse such as Harvard, INSEAD, The University of Western Ontario, Thunderbird, or other organizations. Case studies focus on real issues, concerns, and experiences of a company in a variety of industries. If used well they are excellent learning devices.

We also use other techniques for learning such as role playing, simulations, viewing, and analyzing short video clips, but the method we believe is most effective method called action learning.

Action Learning

Lifetime learning is a key characteristic of the requirements of all people today. Our experience confirms the value of action learning, an instructional strategy that promotes learning by doing. This action by the learners occurs during and after any formalized class or education setting.

Action learning includes:

- *Input* from the instructor, guest speakers from the class or training group, from audio–visual aids, handouts, or pre-assigned readings.
- *Interaction*, which is discussion of the content.
- Data-gathering *instruments* that collect information or opinions for analysis and reflection.

Learning also occurs *after* the group experience in two ways. The first takes place when the learner develops specific action plans at the end of each session; for example, if a learner writes down individual activities he or she plans to engage in or try as a result of the learning. This can be done at the end of a learning module or end of the day of training.

When action learning is used in our leading global projects programs, we as faculty are primarily facilitators, not information distributors. This is based on the beliefs articulated by the guru of adult education Malcolm Knowles who clarified the following related to adult learning in his classic work *The Adult Learner: A Neglected Species.*

- Adults enter a learning activity with an image of themselves as self-directing, responsible grown-ups, not immature, dependent learners; they learn better in a threat-free learning climate that fosters acceptance, freedom, and participation. As faculty we say we want to "create a comfortable, yet challenging atmosphere where leaders of global projects will be willing to question, share, learn, and change."
- Adults enter a learning activity with more experience than young learners, so they have a broader basis for new learning.
- Adults enter a learning activity with more immediate intentions to apply the learning to work or life problems.

Action learning is a dynamic process that is appropriate to mature learners as it simulates learning at both the cognitive and affective levels.

In summary, the principal value of action learning is that it is designed to promote positive and constructive change in people and their organizations through increased awareness, knowledge, and skills.

Imperative 1

Individual action planning.

At the end of our program, we also believe that taking between 15 and 20 minutes to summarize the key points is critical. We have developed an individual action learning plan that assists learners with this task. The following is an example that can also be used by readers of this book when they have completed all 10 chapters.

My Name_____

Personal Action Plan

Visions
Without
Actions
Are
Hallucinations

Personal Action Plan

_____

A. My most important learnings from the book "Leading
    Global Projects" are:

1. _____

_____

2. _____

_____

3. _____

_____

4. _____

_____

B. All leaders of global projects need mentors. Identify your mentors
    (i.e., people you learn from or people who will coach you).

_____

_____

_____

_____

_____

_____

What is the most important quality your mentors or coaches
have that you would like to possess more of?

_____

_____

_____

_____

_____

_____

C. Please identify leaders of global projects who are highly skillful at motivating others.

_____

_____

_____

_____

_____

What do they do to motivate people?

_____

_____

_____

_____

_____

D. Please identify leaders of global projects who are highly skillful in developing trust in team members.

_____

_____

_____

_____

_____

What do they do to develop trust in others?

_____

_____

_____

_____

_____

_____

E.   As a leader of a global project and as a result of reading our book "Leading Global Projects," list six behavioral changes that you intend to enact. Three should be behaviors that you will display more; the other three should be behaviors that you will display less.

I will do *more* of:

1.   _____

2.   _____

3.   _____

I will do *less* of:

1.   _____

2.   _____

3.   _____

F.   Write a brief (two or three sentences) personal vision statement.

_____

_____

_____

_____

Write a vision statement relevant to your role as a leader on a global project.

_____

_____

We end with a quotation from Larry Bossidy:

You won't remember when you retire what you did in the first quarter of 1994 or the third. What you'll remember is how many people you developed, how many people you helped have a better career because of your interest and your dedication to their development…When confused as to how you're doing as a leader, find out how the people you lead are doing. You'll know the answer.

Learning Logs

One of the most effective methods to assist learning is to identify key learnings and retain key points for application in a device we have called a learning log. This is not completed at the end of a program but after each session, before transitioning to another subject with either the same or different faculty member. We ask participants in our leading global projects programs to take out their learning logs. These are in the overleaf of their binders. We ask the learners to reflect on the last session and write what for each were their key learning points. For the thousands of individuals who we have asked to do this we have never had any persons say the exercise was not a very valuable use of time. In fact many in the evaluations completed at the end of the program, say that this document will be where they "capture" individual learnings and ideas to "take back to work." The following learning log can be used by readers of this book following each chapter. A sample is as follows.

Imperative 2

Chapter Learning Log

*Chapter*_____

Based on your reading of the material, please respond to the two questions which follow.

1. What were the key learning points of the chapter?

(a) _____

_____

_____

(b) _____

_____

_____

(c) _____

_____

_____

(d) _____

_____

_____

(e) _____

_____

_____

_____

2. How will the knowledge and/or ideas that you gained from the chapter help you become a more skillful global leader?

(a) _____

_____

_____

(b) _____

_____

_____

(c) _____

_____

_____

_____

Conclusion

We have found the learning logs and the action planning activity effective ways to ensure that the "return on investment" is significant for the individual and the organization. At the end of the 4 or 5 day program on leading global projects we believe it is a waste of the learners time and a waste of the organization's funds if the learnings are not internalized in the individual and subsequently incorporated into the organization.

Capturing the Learning Imperatives

1. Complete an action plan.

2. Keep a journal/learning log of best ideas.

Remember

Visions

Without

Actions

Are

Hallucinations

10

Mindstretching Question, Summary, and Epilogue

Before beginning with a summary of the many points covered in our book, we ask readers to consider the following mindstretching question.

Mindstretching Question

Do theories of American, European, and Japanese leadership/communication apply abroad? Are theories of leadership rooted in culture?

The material in Table 10.1 is taken, with permission from management training materials prepared by US nationals for use in other cultures. Mindstretching question: Are the eight behaviors listed on the left hand column universal "behaviors that help build a trust climate?" Do they apply to some other cultures? All other cultures? Are they universal? Read carefully the eight behaviors.

Here are some "reflections" on the material in Table 10.1 from a Middle East perspective.

- It is stated that an open and natural expression of doubt, concern, and feelings would facilitate a climate of trust. This may be so from a Western perspective, but it might become a barrier to effective communication in the Middle East. Middle Easterners are sensitive, especially when it comes to the expression of doubt and concern in an open manner, in a nonfamiliar setting. Middle Easterners value honesty, but tact is extremely important when expressing disagreement.
- The management style in the Middle East tends to be much more authoritative than in the United States. This is a cultural characteristic that can be explained by the following:
    1. Governments in the Middle East generally are much more authoritative than governments in the West, with the absolute authority being vested in the hands of the ruling class.
    2. The social structure – older persons are highly respected in the Middle East: this stems from religious teachings.
    3. The manager in the Middle East enjoys power and authority. Possessing power and authority in the Middle East is generally relished by those who possess it.

Table 10.1 Managing Climate

Behaviors That Help Build a Trust Climate	Behaviors That Help Preclude a Trust Climate
1. Express your doubts, concerns, and feelings in an open, natural way. Encourage your subordinates to do so also.	1. Look on expressions of feelings and doubts as signs of weakness.
2. When subordinates express their doubts, concerns, and feelings, accept them supportively and discuss them thoroughly.	2. Be sarcastic, but cleverly so.
	3. Let your subordinates know that you expect them to "stretch the truth" a little if it will make the organization look good.
3. Set honesty as one standard that will not be compromised. Demand it from yourself and from your staff.	4. Be secretive. Never let them really be sure what's on your mind. This keeps them on their toes.
4. Be clear about your expectations when assigning work or eliciting opinions. Explain your reasons, whenever possible, behind requests and directions.	5. Discourage subordinates from coming to you for help. After all, they should be "stem-winders" and "self-starters."
5. Encourage subordinates to look to you as a possible resource in accomplishing results, but develop and reinforce independence.	6. When something goes wrong, blow up, hit the ceiling, and look for the guilty party.
6. When something goes wrong, blow up and determine what happened, not "who did it."	7. Gossip about and disparage others on the staff when they are not present. Over respond to casual comments by others about your people.
7. Encourage active support and participation in corrective measures from those involved.	8. Take credit for successes. Plan vendettas and other ploys to make other organizations look bad. Draw on subordinates to carry these out. Always insist on plenty of documentation to protect yourself.
8. Share credit for successes; assume the bulk of responsibility for criticism of your unit.	

Note: Used with permission. Parts are omitted to preserve continuity. These sections are direct excerpts from the training materials of a multinational corporation whose name shall remain anonymous for obvious reasons of critique.

- Although honesty is highly regarded in the Middle East, it is coupled with the concept of saving face and preserving one's honor. Honesty is also a word that has many meanings depending on the situation.
- Clarity in expectations is extremely important. It is very difficult to read another person's mind, but stating clearly what another wants is Western. Another way would be to anticipate the needs or expectations of another (e.g., as Middle Easterners often do).
- When things go wrong, it is sometimes necessary to tell someone that an error was made by an individual in the organization, but this must be done very tactfully.
- To the authors it is evident from the foregoing comments that the training material as presented is generally inappropriate for use in other cultures, in this case the Middle East, because it is based on American cultural assumptions and values. So, the following questions arise:
- Is the material appropriate for international management training?
- Is it appropriate for training Americans to communicate effectively with people in host cultures, such as in the Middle East?
- Is the material appropriate for training Middle Eastern personnel to communicate with Americans? *Yes, if we assume that the Middle Easterners are willing, in order to communicate with Americans, to communicate like Americans. But this is not usually the case.*

"We all have the capacity to inspire and empower others. But we must first and foremost devote ourselves to our personal development and growth as leaders."[1]

We recently interviewed a senior executive from a large pharmaceutical company. He told us he has been "leading projects all my life." Now he is "leading super projects." This leader of super

---

[1]"Discovering Your Authentic Leadership," by Bill George, Peter Sims, Andrew N. McLean, and Diana Mayer, Harvard Business Review, February 2007.

projects never intended to be involved in project management. He was an accidental project leader. He was trained as a physician and scientist.

Another executive who has been observing leaders and managers of projects for many years drew a diagram on a white board which we reproduce. At one end of the continuum, he said there are leaders of global projects who can hardly "read and write." On the other end, there are leaders of projects who can "walk on water." Most are in between.

Skills of Leaders of Global Projects

1   2   3   4   5   6   7   8   9   10

They can   They can
"read and write"   "walk on water"

Our book is directed to the individual who has good skills and knowledge but who wants to get better and improve as a leader. Our book is not directed to an individual who wants to gain more "technical knowledge" about project management. There are many books and courses that are available to help in the important area of project management fundamentals.

Summary

This is a brief summary of the highlights we have covered by chapter.

Chapter 1: Leading Global Projects
- James as an "accidental project leader"
- Projects and strategy
- Projects and culture
- Culture is learned and is complex and changes
- Culture under stress "trumps" all
- The importance of being "bilingual" in low/high context communication in leading projects

Chapter 2: Fundamentals for Project Leaders
- What are "projects"?
- "Elevator speech"
- Project leaders and time management
- Airbus case and risk management
- Projects and strategic value
- Transparency and assumptions in projects
- Project scope, schedule, and charter
- Making "unknowns" known
- Critical path and budget

Chapter 3: Project Leadership
- The "what–why" dance
- The project vision
- The project team
- What's in it for me (WIIFM) imperative
- Project alignment
- Project punch lines
- Project "stories"

Chapter 4: Cross-Cultural/Cross-Functional Skills
- Guss Hiddink and soccer
- Ann Landers – a mistake resulting from cultural filters
- Stereotyping and projects
- Mini-cases of errors…and a framework to understand
- Handling two swords at the same time
- English as the language of global projects

Chapter 5: Influencing and Negotiating
- Project alignment through influencing without authority
- A case of failure in relationship
- Developing and influencing strategy
- What are our "currencies"
- Relationships in the end count most
- A framework for global negotiating
- "Passport to negotiating success"
- Dealing with "conflicts" on projects

Chapter 6: Leaders and Project Teams
- A case of failure
- What team members need from the leader
- Multitasking makes us "stupid"
- Max and his bad attitude
- Motivation and performance
- Bad news does not improve with age
- Empathy and "troublemakers" on global projects
- Virtual teams

Chapter 7: Leading Projects at the Edge of Chaos
- Formal project management impeding the progress of organizations at the edge of chaos
- Small pockets of chaos inflicting tremendous damage
- Seemingly inconsequential initial conditions leading to complex and unpredictable project outcomes
- Identifying early warning signs to avoid pockets of chaos
- The perfect storm of project management
- The critical three questions
- Simplifying

Chapter 8: Change
- No one likes change … not even monkeys
- Change as a way of life
- A model for change
- The change process
- An exercise to initiate successful change
- Change and courage
- Change and risk

Chapter 9: Capturing the Learnings
- Moving from "say to do" and from "talk to walk" and from "knowledge to action"
- A learning exercise
- Learning logs
- Final statement "visions without actions are hallucinations"

Epilogue

We would like to offer a few concluding comments on becoming a "walk on water" project leader.

First and foremost, we must commit ourselves to growing/changing/learning as a leader of global projects.

Second, we have to be keenly aware of our inner compass that guides our behavior as a leader. Self awareness and emotional intelligence are ingredients.

And finally as leaders we have to become increasingly transparent and authentic.

We hope reading this book will contribute to your growth and development as a leader of global projects.

Robert T. Moran
William E. Youngdahl

A Short List of Highly Recommended Books

On Leadership

Shackleton's Way, Morrell, M. and Capparell, S. Penguin Books, 2001.

On Culture and Leadership

Managing Cultural Differences, Moran, R. Harris, P. and Moran, S. Elsevier, 2007.

On Change

The Dance of Change, Senge, P. Currency, 1999.

On Globalization

The World is Flat, Friedman, T. Farrar, Straus and Giroux, 2006.

Bound Together: How Traders, Preachers, Adventurers and Warriors Shaped Globalization, Chanda, N. Yale University Press, 2007.

On Project Management

Project Management: The Managerial Process, Forth Edition, Gray, C. and Larson, E., McGraw-Hill, 2007.

A Guide to the Project Management Body of Knowledge, Third Edition, Project Management Institute, 2004.

On Influencing

Influencing Without Authority, Cohen, A. and Bradford, D. John Wiley and Sons, 2005

Index